Decorative Finishes

by Susan Goans & Jane Gauss

©2004 Plaid Enterprises, Inc., Norcross, GA 30091-7600
www.plaidonline.com • 800-842-4197
PRINTED IN U.S.A.

DISCLAIMER: the information in this instruction book is presented in good faith, but no warranty is given, nor results guaranteed, nor is freedom from any patent to be inferred. Since we have no control over physical conditions surrounding the application of information herin contained, Plaid Enterprises, Inc. disclaims any liability for untoward results.

IMPORTANT: Please be sure to thoroughly read the instructions for all products used to complete projects in this book, paying particular attention to all cautions and warnings shown for that product to ensure their proper and safe use.

COPYRIGHT: All rights Reserved. No part of this book may be reproduced in any form without permission in writing, except by reviewer, who may in reviewing this publication, quote brief passages in a magazine or newspaper.

You don't need a professional to achieve BEAUTIFUL painted finishes on walls and accessories! **It's easy** to create rooms that reflect YOUR PERSONAL STYLE with stenciling, faux finishing, and stamping. Whether your tastes are modern, traditional, or somewhere in between, this book will teach you the techniques for creating **professional results**—with detailed instructions, step-by-step photographs, and tips on choosing color and design themes.

Let the ideas in this book **inspire** you as you create spectacular results—and most of all, **enjoy the fun** of doing it yourself!

INTRODUCTION

about the authors

Jane Gauss

has been stenciling for many years and continues to find new and exciting ways to share her love for stenciling with people around the world. Her obsession with and love for stenciling began as a hobby. It was an affordable means of personalizing and decorating her family's home during years when her husband's career kept the family moving and her two children were small.

After stenciling her family's home, Jane began sharing her love of stenciling with neighbors and friends. Soon she began teaching others to stencil and scheduling custom jobs.

In 1980, the Gauss family moved to Ohio and planted more permanent roots, and Jane set up a classroom in her home to teach stenciling. In 1983, she joined Plaid Enterprises, Inc. as an author and designer. At Plaid, Jane has been instrumental in the development of the Stencil Decor® and Elegant Home™ stenciling programs and is a co-designer of Decorator Blocks® and Stamp Decor. As part of J & L Design, she is also co-designer of PaperIllusion® Sculptured Stone Plaster and MetalWorks. Jane has produced instructional videos and has been a regular guest on QVC, "For Your Home" and "Paint, Paint, Paint" (PBS and TLC). For a time, she also operated a stenciling and faux finish supplies wholesale distributing and mail order company, The Stenciler's Emporium.

Now that their children are in homes of their own, she and her husband are enjoying time at their summer home on Lake Chautauqua in New York and their winter home in Florida. And as the years have shown, Jane continues to teach and share the joy of home decorating with everyone she meets.

Susan Kay Goans

(formerly Driggers) has built a fascinating career out of her love for color and design. In the early 80s, Susan was inventing wall stenciling techniques at a time when stencils were not readily available. Since then, she has perfected technical processes for marbleing and other beautiful faux finishes. Susan continues to create new products and innovative tools. Currently, Susan is working in her private studio, producing a signature series of stencil designs and decorative stamps for Plaid that have a vintage feel. The patterns compliment any style and décor and will be an exciting addition to her portfolio.

Over the years Susan's innovative and inspirational ideas have captured the public eye through the efforts of Plaid Enterprises, a global home décor and craft manufacturing and marketing company. On television, Susan is featured time and again as a specialist in home decorating finishes. She is featured on TV shows such as, The Christopher Lowell Show (Discovery Channel), Kitty Bartholomew (HGTV), Remodeling and Decorating Today, Home Bodies, Home Matters (HGTV), The Beverly DeJulio Show, Your Home Studio and the Easy Does It series.

The creative and deeply personal interest that Susan exhibits in her craft has generated a thriving business. She has authored forty instructional books for the "Do It Yourself" industry and her work has also appeared in numerous consumer and trade magazines. These major magazine publishers generate a vast number of articles over the years, building an abundant portfolio of beautiful accomplishments.

INTRODUCTION

table of contents

Introduction 3

Stenciling 16

Faux Finishing 58

Stamping 102

Photo Gallery 124

Glossary 128

INTRODUCTION

planning design and color

Planning, designing, and choosing colors for a room can be a challenge. The rewards of the process are many, but in the end, creating a room décor by combining elements old and new will bring a sense of accomplishment and satisfaction. Treasured items can be integrated with new furniture, fresh colors and patterns to create the room of your dreams. Whether your decorative finish is stenciled, stamped, faux finished, or a combination, this section will help you with ideas for planning colors, textures and patterns that reflect your personal style—and the confidence you need to put it all together.

Choosing Color

Color is one of our most important means of expression. It can affect our moods and influence our desire to spend time in a room. When choosing colors for a room, consider your personal preferences and those of other household members. Also, consider the style of the room and its use when deciding on color.

Warm colors such as reds, yellows and oranges can be stimulating and create a sense of joy and heightened energy. Cooler hues such as blues and greens are more restful and relaxing. But our response to color is completely individual. You may love a bright and cheerful kitchen; others may prefer the order and simplicity conveyed by black and white. A cozy den may be green, taupe and other natural shades in your home, but your neighbor may prefer blue with splashes of other colors thrown in for fun.

When choosing color, always remember that there are no right or wrong combinations. The most fashionable and fresh ideas come from you.

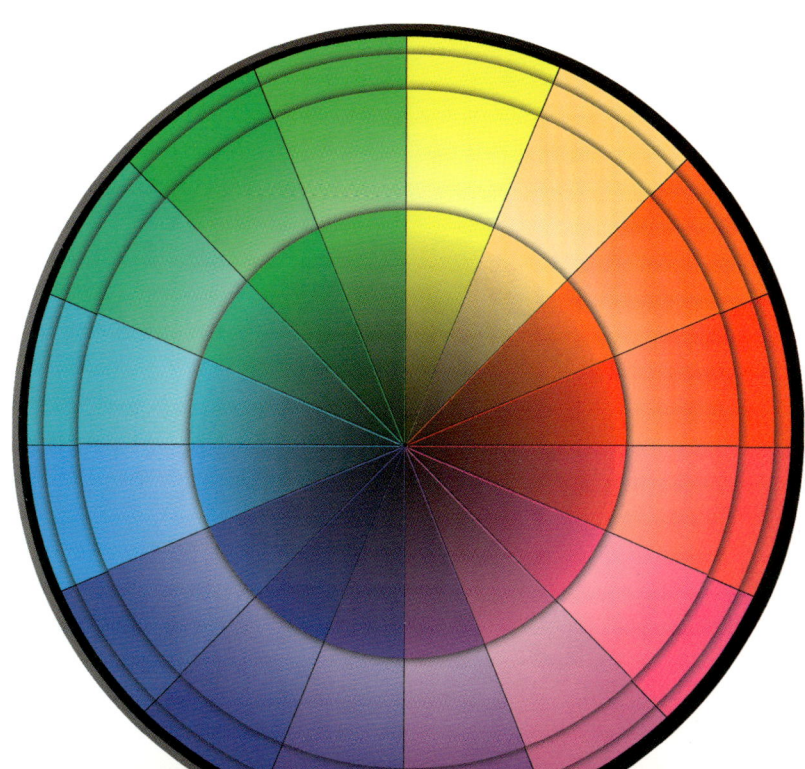

DECORATIVE FINISHES | 9

INTRODUCTION

planning design and color (continued)

Bedrooms

A private retreat, a place of repose—the bedroom offers peace at day's end. A bedroom's style should reflect the personality of the individual or couple who sleeps there. Choose colors that please you and that suit the room's size, shape, and the amount of light it receives. For an old-fashioned, Victorian look, choose deep, antique colors combined with rich velvet and brocade.

Living Areas

Whatever your style, living areas should convey the personality of your home to all who gather there. Choose colors and patterns that are comfortable and agreeable to the family as a whole. A natural color scheme, combined with neutral fibers and textures, are visually appealing and perform well in high-traffic areas.

Formal Areas

Foyers, dining rooms, and living rooms are usually much more formal than the rest of the home and reflect a sense of beauty and elegance. Create the character of these rooms with rich colors and textures as well as dramatic patterns. Creamy white walls offer a warm feel; the addition of plaid silks, sheer fabrics, and extravagant trim will add elegance and formality.

Bedrooms

Living areas

Formal areas

10 | DECORATIVE FINISHES

planning design and color (continued)

Kitchens
Ever notice that at a party, everyone gathers in the kitchen? Today's kitchens can be playful, formal, old fashioned, or retro. Mix fun with function by brightening this key room—for instance, a blue and white color scheme gives a unified look. Fruit, such as grapes or lemons, reminds us of the bounty of the harvest and is especially suited for the kitchen.

Bathrooms
Bathrooms are a wonderful place to showcase playful colors that might not be chosen in another room. Make a bold impression with darker colors and oversized patterns—for instance, a purple color scheme dresses up a plain white-walled bathroom.

Kitchens

Bathrooms

INTRODUCTION

tools and materials

Whether you create a decorative finish using stencils, faux finishing or stamps, the right tools can make all the difference. Choose quality brushes, paints and accessories for professional results—every time.

Stenciling

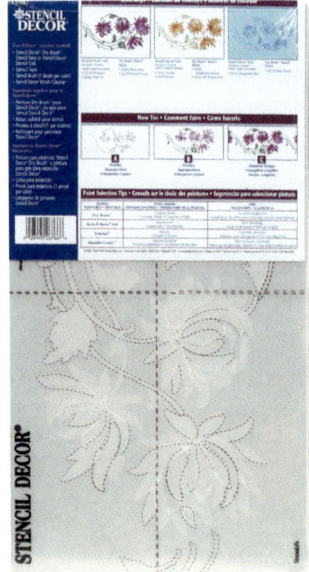

Stencils

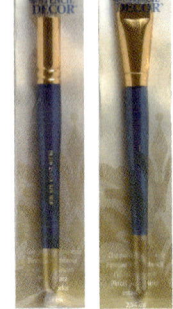

Brushes

Spouncer™

Stencil Roller

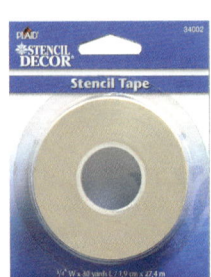

Stencil Tape

Daubers

Stencil Cutter

12 DECORATIVE FINISHES

INTRODUCTION

tools and materials (continued)

Faux Finishing

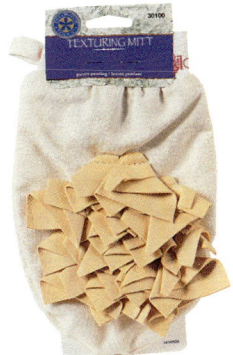
Texturing Mitt

Ragging Mitt

Mopping Mitt

Sponging Mitt

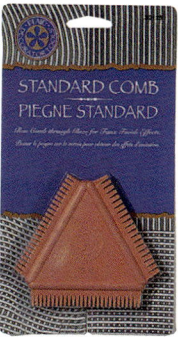
Standard Comb

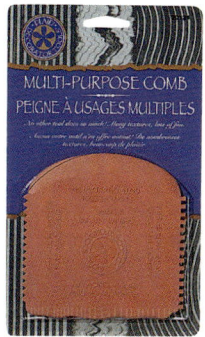
Multi-Purpose Comb

Wall Weaver

Stippler Brush

French Brush

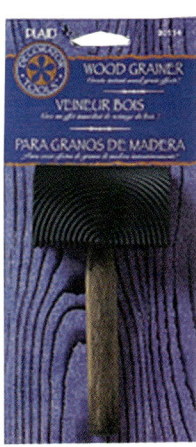
Wood Grainer

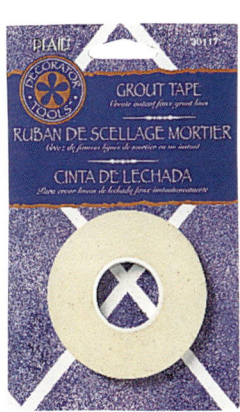
Grout Tape

Sponges

DECORATIVE FINISHES | 13

INTRODUCTION

tools and materials (continued)

Stamping

Foam Stamps

Glaze Roller

Brushes

Choosing Paint for Your Project

Stencil Gel
Stencil Gel is a quick-drying, translucent paint that can be used to create delicate shading and depth. Stencil Gel can be applied using a brush, sponge or roller.

Dry Brush™ Stencil Paint
Dry Brush Stencil Paint is a creamy, solid paint that offers easy, no-mess stenciling. Colors blend beautifully and won't run under stencil edges. Dry Brush Paint is applied using a stencil brush.

CreamStix™ Paint
CreamStix Paint features a space-saving twist-up container that holds a room-size amount of Dry Brush paint.

FolkArt® Acrylic Colors
FolkArt Acrylic Colors are thick, creamy, high-quality paints that can be used for stenciling and stamping. A wide range of color choices make FolkArt paint ideal for any project.

Decorator Glaze
Decorator Glaze is a waterbased, non-toxic gel that's perfect for stamping and faux finishing. It is often used to tint Neutral Wall Glaze for covering larger areas.

Neutral Wall Glaze
Neutral Wall Glaze is perfect for creating faux finishes on walls, furniture and other large areas, Neutral Wall Glaze can be tinted with Decorator Glaze or any latex paint. Glaze stays wet on surface allowing time to create faux effects with various tools and color combinations. Dries to a hard satin finish.

Stencil Gel

Dry Brush™ Stencil Paint

CreamStix™

FolkArt® Acrylic Paint

Neutral Wall Glaze and Decorator Glaze

14 | DECORATIVE FINISHES

surface preparation

Previously Painted Dry Wall
Clean surface to remove grease or dirt. Wash and rinse with clear water. Let dry 24-36 hours. Apply a flat latex primer if the wall color is to be changed drastically from dark to light. Apply 1-2 coats of wall color.

New or Repaired Drywall
Remove dust and dirt with the soft brush attachment of a vacuum cleaner. Apply 1-2 coats of flat latex drywall primer (primer can be tinted to the same tone as the wall color). Let dry. Apply 2 coats of wall color.

Unpainted Plaster
Sand as necessary. Dust with broom or soft brush attachment of a vacuum cleaner. Apply 1 coat of polyvinyl acrylic primer. Let dry. Apply 2 coats of wall color.

Previously Painted or Old Plaster
Clean to remove any grease or dirt. Wash and rinse with clear water. Let dry 24-36 hours. Fill any cracks with vinyl spackling paste. Let dry. Sand and clean spackled surface. Prime with polyvinyl acrylic primer when painting over a dark color or if you're not sure what type of paint was first used. Apply 2 coats of wall color.

Wooden Surfaces
Sanding is usually needed to prepare wooden surfaces for painting. Sand the surface until it feels smooth, sanding in the direction of the grain. Wipe the surface with a tack cloth to remove dust. (A tack cloth is a piece of cheesecloth that has been treated with a mixture of varnish and linseed oil and is very sticky.) Base paint and add any other background finishes. Let dry.

Fabrics
Prewash and dry fabric to remove the sizing that comes in new fabric. This will help the paint bond better with the fibers. Place and secure the fabric over a piece of plastic-covered or waxed cardboard to create a firm surface for stenciling and to prevent bleed-through to any other part of the fabric.

Before you begin, take time to prepare the surface that you'll be painting. A properly prepared surface is easier to work with and will give a better end result.

HELPFUL HINTS:
- Patch cracks, holes, or imperfections with spackling compound.
- Wash surfaces—especially those in bathrooms and kitchens – to remove grease, wax, dirt, and other contaminants.
- Rinse thoroughly to remove all traces of soap.
- Dull glossy surfaces by sanding lightly. Wipe with a damp cloth to remove dust.
- Smooth patched areas by sanding lightly.

STENCILING

Stenciling is the process of applying paint through cutout areas of a material that is impervious to paint. Through the ages, stenciling has provided ornamentation while offering a means of artistic self-expression. Evidence of stenciling can be traced back to the beginning of recorded time, and the popularity of this versatile decorative finish continues today.

With stenciling, a hand-painted look can be created on almost any surface, including walls, floors, floor cloths, fabric, wood, and accessories. In this section, you'll learn about types of stencils, the tools and supplies needed, and a variety of techniques for applying color to create borders, overall patterns, and more.

With a little practice, you'll soon be creating your own professional-looking results! Enjoy, and let your personal style develop as you learn this satisfying and rewarding technique.

STENCILING

tools and materials

Stenciling supplies come in all shapes and sizes—to say that any one is better than another would be inaccurate. Each stenciler develops a style through the types of tools they use. For example, a stenciler quickly personalizes each project based on these tools and the techniques they incorporate. Each tool gives a different "look" and each "look" becomes a signature of the individual stenciler.

Following is an overview of the basic supplies you'll need to begin stenciling. Most can be purchased at craft retailers or in the decorating departments of hardware and home center stores.

Stencils

Ready-made, pre-cut stencils are available for purchase; in addition, many stencilers cut their own designs using a craft knife or stencil cutter. Stencils can be made from nearly any material, including oiled paper, metal, plastic sheets and other transparent materials such as polyester film, acetate, and Mylar.

Interesting effects can also be created using non-traditional stencils—try creating designs with masking tape, paper doilies, fabric and paper lace and natural materials such as leaves or petals.

Every stencil has two components – windows, which are the opening or cut out areas through which paint is applied; and bridges, which are the parts of the stencil that separate the openings.

Brushes and Paint Applicators

There are all shapes and sizes of traditional stencil brushes. The short, dense bristles are designed to distribute paint evenly and prevent the paint from oozing beneath the stencil. Brushes are typically round; however, the style or shape of the brush can vary and can offer an effective stroke variety. Rollers, foam daubers, Spouncers™, cellulose and natural sea sponges also offer effective application tools, depending on the finished look desired.

Paints

Select a stencil paint that matches your stenciling style as well as the surface you are working with. Virtually any type of paint can be used for stenciling, so let permanency, transparency, sheen, etc. be your guide to the best paint for the project. (See page 14 for details on paints.)

Additional Tools and Materials

- Paper or foam plates for a disposable and readily accessible palette
- Paper towels for offloading paint
- Chalk pencil for marking fabrics and walls
- Low-tack masking tape to hold stencil to surface
- Yardstick, measuring tape, bubble (carpenter's) level and plumb line.
- Ladder

18 DECORATIVE FINISHES

STENCILING

making stencils

Stencil blanks are a convenient way to cut your own stencil designs. Stencil Decor® Stencil Blanks are marked with centering lines and are easy to cut using a craft knife or electric stencil cutter.

Gather the Following Supplies:
✓ Plate glass with sanded or rounded edges
   OR a self-healing cutting mat
✓ Fine tip permanent marker
✓ Stencil Blanks
✓ Craft knife or electric stencil cutter

Trace the Design
(Photo A)
Position the stencil blank over the design to be traced. Leave a border of stencil material at least 1" wide around the design. Trace the design with a fine tip permanent marker. If the design requires multiple overlays, trace the design motifs for each overlay with solid lines. Use dotted lines to show the position of motifs that will be cut from other overlays. Using a light table for tracing is recommended (You can make your own light table by putting a lamp under a glass top table.)

OPTIONAL: Instead of tracing the design, hand feed the stencil blanks through a copy machine. After cutting, add registration marks with a permanent pen.

Cutting Designs Using a Craft Knife
(Photo B)
Place the stencil blank on a cutting surface. Plate glass is an ideal surface as the blade moves easily around curved areas. Using a craft knife with a sharp, sturdy blade, hold the knife as you would a pencil and rest the heel of your hand on the cutting surface. Start by cutting a simple shape, applying enough pressure so the tip of the blade cuts the stencil blank and makes contact with the glass. Work slowly, using your fingers to move the knife, resting the heel of your cutting hand on the surface. Use your other hand to move the stencil so you are always cutting toward yourself. Don't lift the blade until the entire shape has been cut. When you come to a point or a curve, lift the heel of your cutting hand so you can turn the stencil blank. When you reach the starting point, turn the stencil so your blade is in its original position. The shape should pop out.

STENCILING

making stencils (continued)

Cutting Designs Using an Electric Cutter
(Photo A)
Place the stencil on a heatproof cutting surface. Hold the cutter as you would a pencil and apply uniform pressure to the stencil, using just enough to cut the material smoothly. Using too much pressure will bend the tip. Trace the design outline, moving around the shape in a continual motion. When you come to a point or a corner, lift the tip. Be sure to read and follow the manufacturer's instructions when using an electric stencil tool!

Cutting Designs Using the Simply® Craft Knife
(Photo B)
The Simply® Craft Knife from Plaid is ideal for cutting smaller stencil designs or for general craft use. To cut a stencil with the Simply Craft Knife, follow the instructions for using a craft knife on page 20.

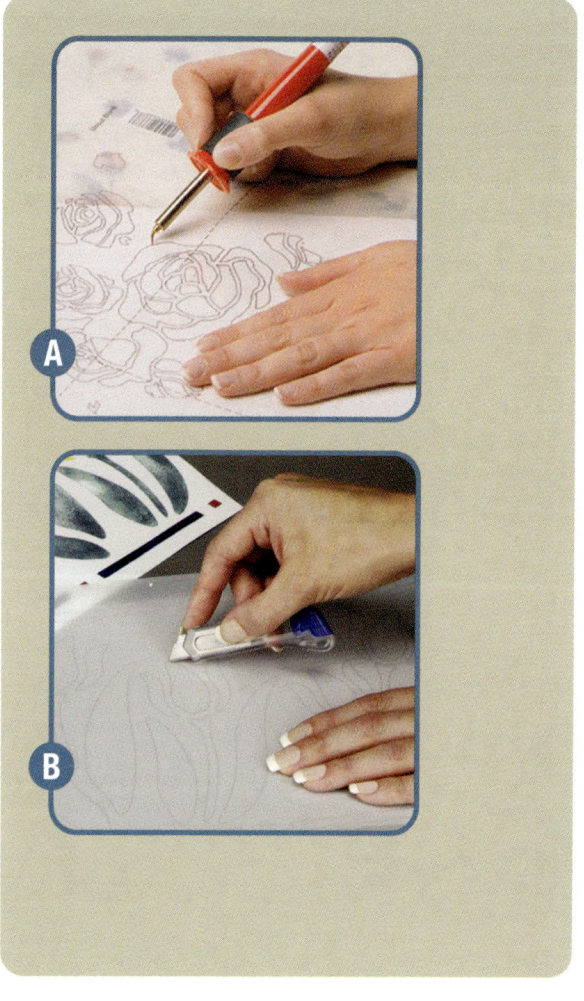

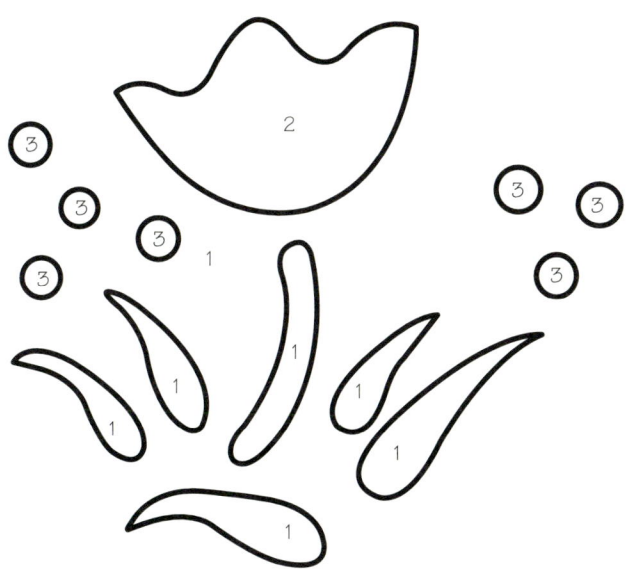

No matter which cutting method you choose, always practice first! Become comfortable with cutting straight lines, curves, sharp points and circles. Above is a simple pattern that teaches all of these angles. You may cut it all on one stencil, or practice overlays and registration markings by cutting stencils #1, 2, and 3. When finished, stencil the design to see how your overlays realign as well as to assess the accuracy of the cutting.

DECORATIVE FINISHES

STENCILING

how to stencil

Once you have selected your paints, brushes and stencil design, you are ready to begin stenciling. Be sure to practice stenciling on paper (see below) before climbing the ladder and attaching the stencil to a wall. Learn how to manage your paints and understand the markings on the stencil so that you feel in total control of the tools you have selected. Review pages 30-32 for specific tips on creating various types of stencil prints, either by paint application, brush technique, or a combination of several techniques. Once you have achieved the look you want, use your practice print as a reference while you work.

Make a Paper Proof
A sample print of the stencil design, or a paper proof, can be used for testing the accuracy of overlays, alignment, color blend with the room's décor, and also the best tool for practicing techniques. Paper proofs are also a measurement tool for judging design placement in corners and around architectural elements. Continuous feed computer paper, shelf paper or the back of freezer paper can all be used to make a proof. Store the proofs with the stencil to make the design more identifiable.

If stenciling on a surface other than white, it's a good idea to paint the proof paper or board with the background color, let dry, then stencil the design.

Loading the Brush
(Photo A)
Squeeze a dime-sized amount of paint or gel on a palette or disposable foam plate, grouping color families together. Holding the brush perpendicular to the palette, pull the bristles through the paint and swirl to concentrate the gel or paint in the center of the brush. Remove excess paint or gel by pouncing and swirling the loaded brush on a paper towel. You are stenciling with a "dry" brush, with outside edges free of paint buildup. The paint is loaded in the center bristles and is released with pressure on the brush during stenciling.

Applying Paint
Work the loaded brush first on an uncut part of the stencil. **(Photo B)** Bring the paint into the cutout area with a light pouncing or circular stroke. **(Photo C)** Use more pressure on the outside edge for a shaded print or use firm pressure over the entire cutout to create an opaque print. (See examples of types of stencil prints, page 32.) To revitalize the brush, use a blending medium or extender. These mediums will extend paint's "open"(wet) time. Do not use water—it will saturate the brush and cause run-unders.

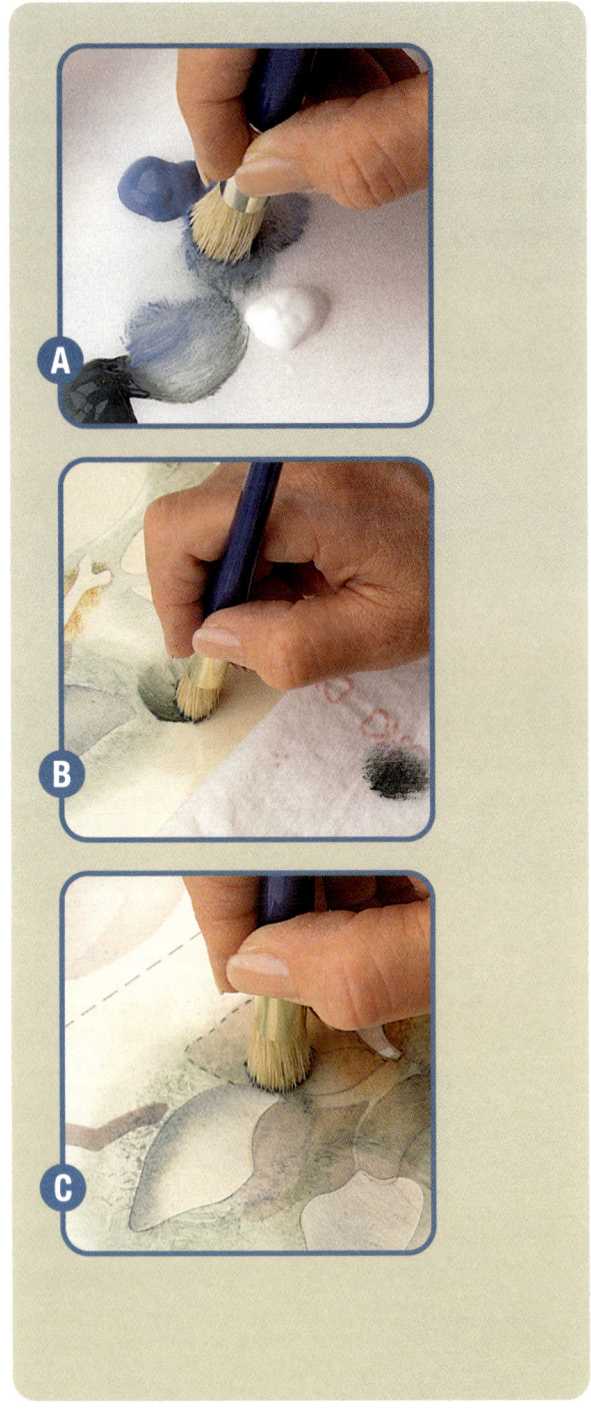

Completed stencil print.

STENCILING

how-to stencil (continued)

STENCILING

spouncing

Daubers and Spouncers™ offer a quick and easy way to apply paint.

Spouncer™
A stenciling sponge on a short wooden handle, the Spouncer fits comfortably in your palm and can be re-used when wet. The Spouncer is available in three sizes: 3/4", 1-1/4", and 1-3/4". The Spouncer can be used with Dry Brush paints, acrylic paints, Stencil Gels or Decorator Glaze.

Daubers
Daubers are applicators with round sponge tips. The wooden handled daubers are available in 5/8" and 1/4" sizes. Daubers are compact and perfect for tight spots.

Stenciling with a Spouncer™ or Dauber
Load palette with small amounts of paints or gels. Place a small amount of blender in the center. Slightly moisten the foam tip with water and blot dry. **(Photo A)** Pull a small amount of paint from the puddle and work into the foam. **(Photo B)** Pounce or swirl paint into the cut out area of the stencil. **(Photo C)** See various stencil strokes on page 33.

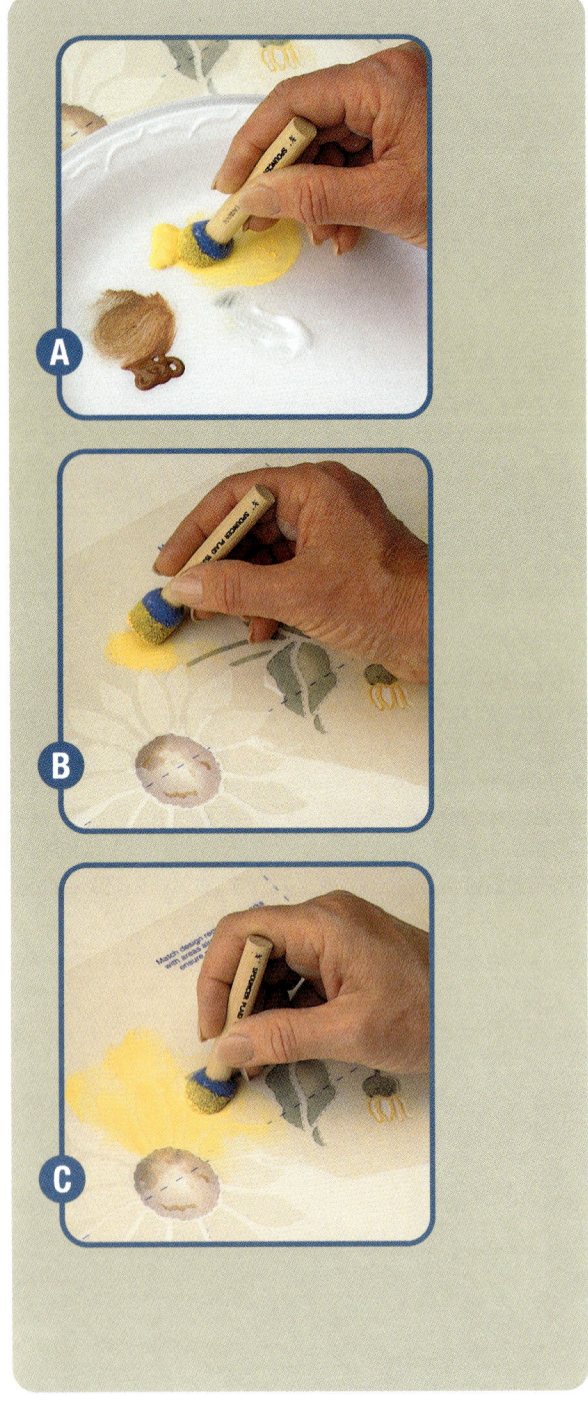

STENCILING

sponging

A lightly moistened sea sponge can be used to create textures and instant blending. A translucent gel or glaze works best. If using an acrylic paint, use a blending gel to meld colors.

Stenciling with a Sponge

Moisten the sponge and blot dry. Place small amounts of several colors onto a palette or disposable foam plate. Pounce one section of sponge in a color, then rotate sponge and pick up another color. Three to four colors can be loaded on one sponge. **(Photo A)** Stencil the design by lightly pouncing the sponge over stencil, going back over the outer edge for definition. Rotate sponge and pounce on another color over the wet paint on surface. **(Photo B)**

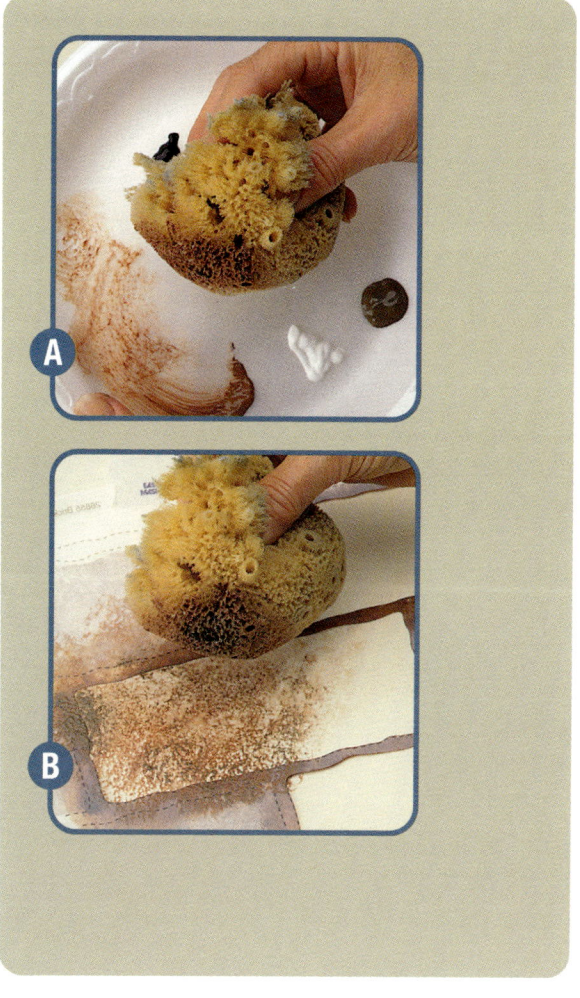

DECORATIVE FINISHES | 25

STENCILING

dry brush paint

Dry Brush paints are applied using a brush. This creamy, solid paint blends beautifully and won't run under stencil edges.

Stenciling with Dry Brush Paint

1. Remove the seal from the dry brush jar by breaking through the seal and removing with a paper towel. Discard paper towel. **(Photo A)**
2. Load the brush by holding the brush as you would a pencil and circle the surface of the paint three to four times. **(Photo B)**
3. Circle the loaded brush on the uncut part of the stencil to disperse the paint. **(Photo C)**
4. Stencil by bringing brush into cut out area with a light circular stroke. Swirl paint on the entire cutout area or around the outer edges of the design. **(Photo D)** Add more pressure to your brush, not more paint, continuing with a clockwise, then counter-clockwise stroke.

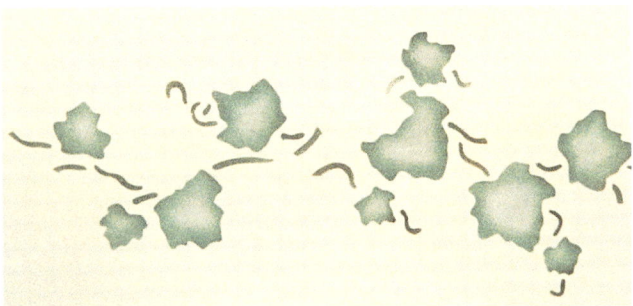

Overlay A

Overlay B

26 | DECORATIVE FINISHES

STENCILING

creamstix

CreamStix paint features a space-saving twist-up container that holds a room-size amount of Dry Brush paint.

Stenciling with Creamstix

1. Twist up paint color and smear a small amount on the uncut part of the stencil (away from the cut area) and pick up paint on the brush. **(Photo A)**
2. Swirl the brush in the paint, then on a paper towel to remove excess. **(Photo B)**
3. Brush paint in stencil cutouts using a light circular stroke. **(Photo C)**

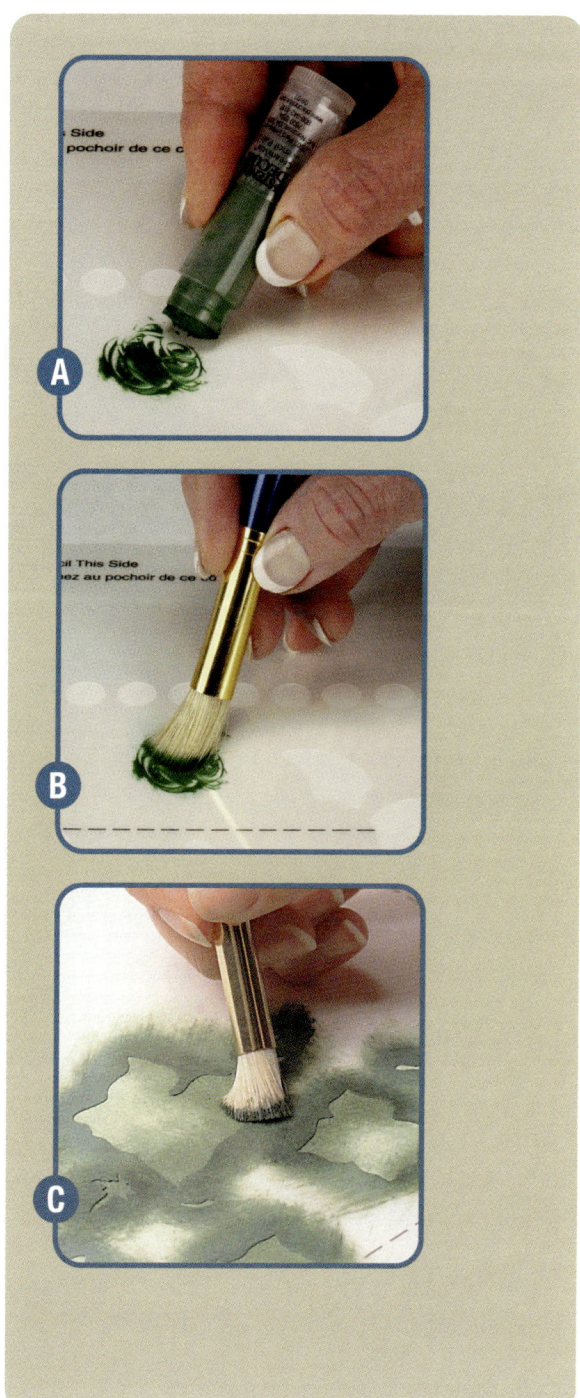

DECORATIVE FINISHES | 27

STENCILING

stencil care

Every stenciler builds a collection of tools that they can control and reuse. Whatever tools you choose, it is imperative that they are properly cleaned and stored after use so they can continue to work for you.

Stencil Saver

Stencil Saver minimizes stencil clean up and dramatically preserves the life of the stencil. Regardless of paint buildup and drying, a pre-treated stencil rinses clean in warm water.

Apply Stencil Saver to a clean, dry stencil and let dry. Stencil as usual. When project is complete, place stencil in a water-filled sink. Rub gently to remove the paint. **(Photo A)** The top half of this stencil was treated with Stencil Saver before use. Notice how easily the dried stencil paint wipes off the stencil.

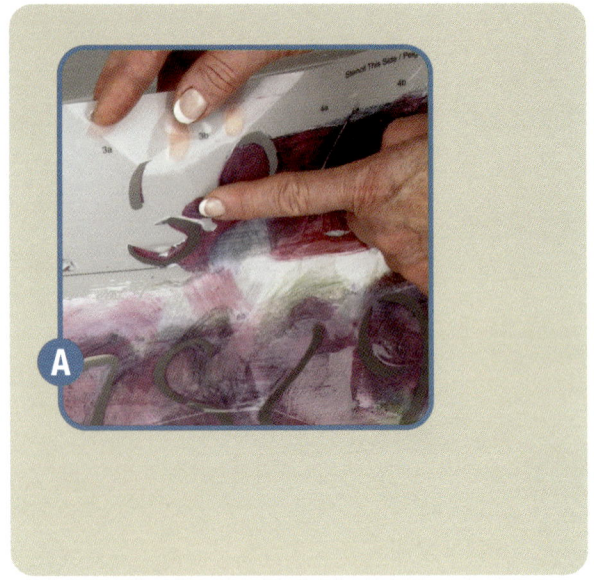

Cleaning Stencils

If your stencil has not been pre-treated with Stencil Saver, be sure to clean it immediately after using. Do not allow the paint to cure on the surface of the stencil.

1. Place stencil in bottom of sink and brush on Stencil Decor Brush Cleaner or Murphy's Oil Soap. Use the stencil brush to gently remove the paint. Rinse clean with water.
2. Gently wipe stencil with pot scrubber cellulose sponge, being careful not to tear the bridges. The longer the paint cures on the stencil, the more difficult cleaning will become.
3. When using Dry Brush paints or Cream Stix, wipe the stencil with a paper towel immediately after use. Brush on Stencil Décor Brush Cleaner or Murphy's Oil Soap. Rinse and dry. If the paint has cured, follow steps 1 and 2 above.

The left half of this stencil was treated with Stencil Saver before use. Notice how easily the dried stencil paint wipes off the stencil.

Storing Stencils

After cleaning, store stencils flat in their original package, or in large envelopes or file folders. Tape a copy of a paper proof to the package or folder for easy design identification.

Repairing Stencils

If your stencil becomes torn, repair it by applying a small amount of transparent tape to both sides of the tear. Use a utility knife to cut away tape from inside the cutout areas of the design.

STENCILING

brush care

Thoroughly clean brushes and rollers at the end of the day. If this is not possible, wrap your tools in a moist paper towel and place in a plastic bag until you can clean them.

Cleaning Brushes
(Photo A)

1. Dip tips of bristles in Stencil Decor Brush Cleaner. To activate cleaner, dip brush in water. Never soak a brush in water.
2. Work the brush on a bristle scrubber or on a pot scrubber. Add more water, if needed, to create a foamy lather. Rinse clean and blot brush on a towel.
3. For larger brushes, loop a rubber band around bristle tips and roll it to the ends of the bristles to keep them from splaying.
4. Place brushes on their sides to dry. When dry, store brushes flat or on the handle ends with bristles up. Brushes should be completely dry before re-use.

Cleaning Foam Brushes and Stencil Rollers

1. Thoroughly clean foam brushes or rollers after use. Do not let paint dry on the roller. While stenciling, keep roller or foam brush from drying out by placing it in a zip-top bag or in plastic wrap.
2. Wash with mild soap and water.
3. Rinse until water runs clear. Let dry. When the roller or foam brush is damp dry, it can be reloaded and used again.

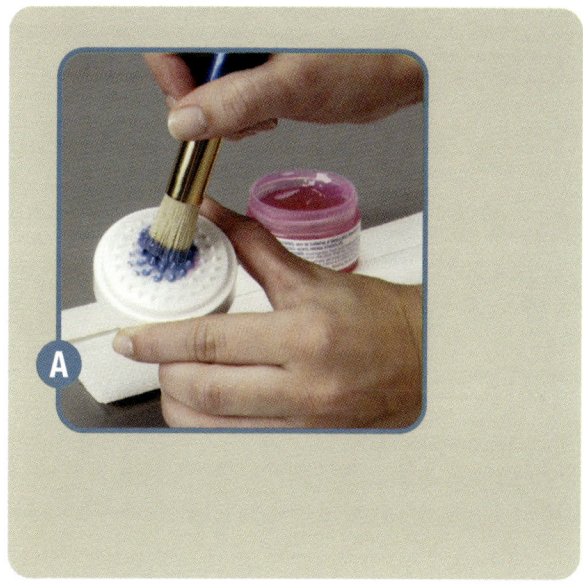

DECORATIVE FINISHES | 29

STENCILING

types of stencils

There are two types of stencils, regardless of the stencil material used. They are single overlay and multiple overlay.

Single Overlay Stencils

Single overlay stencils have bridges between cut out areas; the complete design is on one sheet. A bridge is the dividing partition within the design. These bridges separate the design elements and hold the stencil together. The more bridges within a stencil, the more fragile it will become and the closer the cut out areas will be to one another. Therefore, the purpose of bridges is twofold: (a) Gives strength to the stencil (b) Separates colors and design elements

Multiple Overlay Stencils

Multiple overlay stencils consist of two or more layers. As the number of overlays increases, the total number of bridges in the final stencil print decreases. With all bridges eliminated, a more realistic hand-painted design is created because the painted areas butt up against each other— rather than being separated by bridges.

A multiple overlay stencil allows for faster paint application when multiple colors are used. One or two colors can be added with each overlay. The overlays are matched with either dotted or printed registration marks or drilled realignment holes that are transferred to the surface. To remove cut areas that don't drop out of a precut Mylar stencil, briskly shake the stencil with a rolling motion. Some stencil designs have drop out pieces attached. To remove, cut on solid lines with scissors or a craft knife. Save the larger drop out pieces to use as templates for shadowing and shading.

Single overlay stencil.

Multiple overlay stencil.

STENCILING

types of stencils (continued)

Theorem Stenciling

Theorem style stencils consist of a series of intricately cut overlays, eliminating space between motif components to produce complex images. With the advent of laser cutting, these precise, highly detailed stencils are becoming accessible and affordable. The term theorem stenciling refers to the design, cutting, and stenciling of intricate, bridgeless prints.

Value, tone, and intensity of color are key elements to effective theorem stenciling. To begin, place each stencil overlay over the full-size color reproduction of the sample print. This will help you to understand which part of the design corresponds to each window. Pay attention to how each area is shaded and refer to the sample print as you stencil to verify the location and intensity of the shading. The overlays are not designated for a specific color but rather for specific design elements. Proper alignment is essential to avoid "halos" – areas within the print where the background shows.

Trompe l'oeil

Trompe l'oeil, French for "fool the eye" (pronounced "tromp loy"), is a style of painting that gives an illusion of reality, hence the size and placement of the design is important. For example, a stenciled flowerpot would be "sitting" on a shelf (either real or stenciled) and not suspended on the wall.

Halos on the stencil print indicate improper alignment of the layers.

To eliminate halo, reposition the overlay and stencil the edge again.

Example of trompe l'oeil stenciling. The bricks look real because of texture created with paint, shadowing, and the scale of the brick itself.

DECORATIVE FINISHES | 31

STENCILING

types of stencils (continued)

Freehand
In the freehand style, decorative painting and stenciling are combined to add shading and highlighting to the finished stencil print. The stenciled design can be used as a base or as the outline for hand painting. With the addition of basic brush strokes, a stencil with bridges can have the look of a bridgeless stencil. Use a round artist's brush with thinned paint when connecting bridges.

Mirror Image
A mirror image stencil is achieved by stenciling on the back or reverse side of the stencil, resulting in a reversed printed image. This is an effective technique for building a central motif, or for creating facing images over doors or windows. Some designs work better than others as mirror images. Test the effectiveness by stenciling the motifs first on paper, then positioning them on the surface to determine balance and spacing.

Stencil Prints
The finished stenciled image is referred to as a print. It is important to make consistent prints; for example, you do not want the print of one overlay to be dark and opaque and the print on the next repeat to be faint.

OPAQUE PRINT: a stencil print with intense color buildup and without tone or variance. This style of print is very effective with bright or primary colors.

TRANSLUCENT PRINT: a stencil print that is lighter toward the center of the design with a shaded, distinct outer edge. On some surfaces, the background surface or texture shows through.

To determine which style best suits your wall, practice stenciling on paper, then tape the proofs in the room you will be stenciling. Adjust the intensity of paint color or application technique to the desired look.

The right side of this stencil print is enhanced with decorative painting.

Using a mirror image to create a central motif.

Using a mirror image to create facing images.

Opaque print.   **Translucent print.**

STENCILING

stencil strokes

A quality stencil print has defined edges and a consistent look. This does not mean that all prints should look exactly the same, but rather that the prints blend with the overall décor theme, and that a flow of design and a balance of color are maintained. Shading, shadowing and remaining consistent with a natural or fictional light source also adds dimension.

Circular
Use a circular stroke to achieve an evenly shaded print. Move the loaded brush in a clockwise or counter clockwise direction, focusing on the outside edge of the cutout area. The circular stroke is recommended when using Dry Brush or Cream Stix paint. If acrylic paints or gels are used, care must be taken to remove excess paint from the brush and to keep a light pressure on the brush to prevent smudged prints.

Pouncing
A pounced stroke is ideal for beginners, as it will not readily cause a smudged print. Apply the paint in an up-and-down pouncing motion. The more you pounce, the more solid or opaque the print will become.

Sweeping
Use a back-and-forth sweeping stroke to create a directional print. This stroke is especially effective in large cut out areas, or when using a flat stencil brush. Use caution—too much paint on the brush can result in a brush-under smudge.

Rolling
The stencil roller can be used with one or two shades of paint on the roller. A darker color can then be added to accent areas of the stencil or for the second overlay. The finished print will not have outside edge shading.

Combination
A combination stroke blends pouncing, circular and sweeping strokes. This secondary stroke added after the stencil print is first rolled on the surface. Then, for example, certain design elements can be pounced with a brush or foam applicator.

Circular strokes.

Pouncing strokes.

Sweeping strokes.

Rolling strokes.

DECORATIVE FINISHES | 33

STENCILING

brush feathering

Brush feathering (sometimes called "fluffing") is used to soften a hard stenciled edge. Brush feathering can give an aged or worn look, or it can be used to create a natural fur or feather look on animals or birds.

Using the Feathering Technique
(Photo A)

To brush feather, stencil the print. Lift the stencil and brush out 1/8" to 1/4" over the still-wet edge with a flat stenciling brush. Be sure to use a very dry brush and practice first. It is essential that the feathering technique, whether used on an edge or an element within the stencil print (such as detail within a leaf) be created with a light touch.

34 DECORATIVE FINISHES

STENCILING

correcting mistakes

Only a few stenciling mistakes cannot be corrected. The worst thing that can happen is that you would need to repaint the wall and start again. Although some smudges can be corrected, continual smudges indicate a technique problem that gives a much more amateur look to a stenciling project.

Brush Over
A brush-over is created when paint is brushed over the edge of the stencil. If there is not enough material around the edge of the stencil, use low tack tape to protect the outside surface. To correct a brush-over, use an artist's eraser to remove the smudge. If the smudge occurs when using Dry Brush paint, press a piece of masking tape over the smudge to remove paint, then carefully erase with the artist's eraser.

Brush Under
A brush-under is created when the bristles go under the stencil, causing a smudge. A brush-under is usually the result of any of the following: (a) A too-wet overloaded brush, combined with too much pressure on the brush or a sweeping stroke with a too-wet brush. (b) Loose stencil—not taping or holding the stencil flat on the surface. (c) Improper focus of vision.

To prevent brush-unders, blot as much paint as you can from the brush onto a paper towel, then begin stenciling with a light pressure to determine the paint pickup on the surface. To remove a brush under, shift the stencil slightly and create a new edge to cover the smudge.

Smudge Removal
To remove a smudge that cannot be hidden, immediately use a pre-moistened wipe or a cotton swab moistened with isopropyl alcohol to remove the stenciled print. Let surface dry, use an artist's eraser to remove any remaining pigment, and re-stencil.

If this method will not remove the smudge, cover the mistake with background paint. When the paint is thoroughly dry, re-stencil.

Prints to Avoid
PAINT TOO WET: This print was stenciled with liquid paint using an overloaded brush and heavy pressure, causing the paint to run under the stencil. Use a very light circular motion to prevent this problem.

PAINT TOO DRY: To correct a print that is too dry, try using a small amount of Blender to rejuvenate the liquid paint in the brush. For Dry Brush paints, reload the brush and work paint into the bristles before stenciling on the cutout area.

UNEVENLY LOADED BRUSH: An unevenly loaded brush can result in paint buildup on the edge of the stencil, causing smudges when the stencil is moved. Whether working with liquid or Dry Brush paint, be sure to work the paint evenly through the bristles before stenciling.

Example of brush over.

Example of brush under.

Paint too wet.

Paint too dry.

Unevenly loaded brush.

DECORATIVE FINISHES | 35

STENCILING

focus of vision

Focus of vision is an important concept that will help you to achieve uniform and balanced stencil prints. For consistency in multiple prints, it is essential for a professional look.

Focus of vision is simply the part of the cut out area your eye is concentrating upon as you apply paint to the cutout area. The edge of the cut stencil gives definition to the design and determines the placement of shading.

By focusing the eye on the tight circular stroke on the outer edge of the design, the outline is defined, and a balanced, shaded print can be created and replicated. This focus of vision is especially important when working with bridgeless or theorem-style stencils. If you are using the brush feathering technique, the focus of vision would be to the center of the cut out area.

This birdhouse has a correct focus, resulting in a balanced, shaded print.

This birdhouse print shows a focus on paint in the center of the cut out area, resulting in a blurry, poorly balanced print.

36　DECORATIVE FINISHES

STENCILING

border styles

Borders are created by repeated elements that form a continuous design and are typically placed at the ceiling line. Borders can also be placed on the ceiling, at chair rail height, or along the base trim molding. Elements from a border design can also be used as free-form elements. Most borders are used horizontally.

Architectural Borders
Architectural borders are composed of elements derived from trim moldings, initially carved in wood or in plaster relief. Created with multiple overlays, a consistent shading is achieved and the design takes on a three-dimensional look.

Ceiling Line Border or Frieze
A ceiling line border or frieze is stenciled at the top of a wall. Allow about an inch from the ceiling line to the top of the design. If there is a crown molding, begin the stencil 1/2" to 1" below the molding trim. For an 8' ceiling, the border should be at least 6" wide.

Mirrored Border
You can create a wider border from a narrow stencil design by doubling it. Use the mirror image placement technique (page 32).

Centered Border
A centered border is created by first stenciling design elements in particular spaces, such as in a corner, centered over a mantel, window or door. The border can then be used to connect the centered elements to the corner.

Architectural border

Ceiling border

Mirrored border

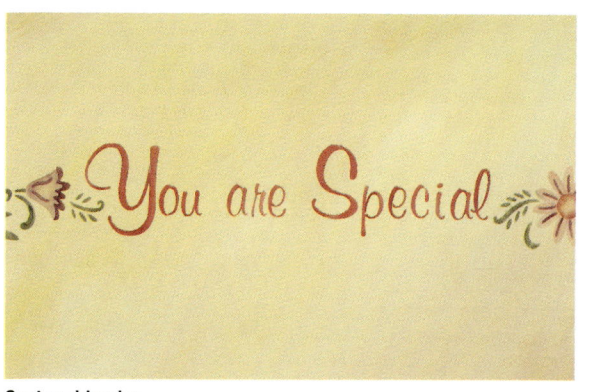

Centered border

DECORATIVE FINISHES | 37

STENCILING

border styles (continued)

Chair Rail Border

This type of border is stenciled at chair rail height. It is usually a narrow border that would mimic the width of wood chair rail molding.

1. Measure 32-36" up from the floor. Use a spirit or bubble level to draw a horizontal line around the room. Mark the line lightly with a chalk pencil.
2. The chair rail must be level, even if the floor is not.
3. Sometimes it is best to allow other elements or furniture in the room to determine the height of a chair rail – for example, in a dining room, place the chair rail at the point where the back of a chair would touch the wall.
4. Align the horizontal centering line printed on the stencil with the chalk markings on the wall. Erase any marks that are in the way of the stencil design.
5. Stencil the design, moving around the room. Let dry.
6. Erase the remaining chalk marks.

Continuous Flowing Border

A continuous flowing border is a series of repeated design elements without straight edges. The longer the stencil sheet, the more "movement" the design will have and the repeat will be more difficult to detect visually. The design elements usually flow in the same direction. Most vine and floral border stencils are continuous flowing border stencils.

Straight Border

A straight border has a definite straight edge at the top and/or bottom of the design. When placing a straight border at the top or bottom of a wall, be sure the ceiling line or base trim is level. To do this, place a spirit or bubble level along the line where the wall meets—either the ceiling or the floor. If the level is off by more than half a bubble, select a flowing border design rather than a straight border, and allow the flowing edge of the border to follow the out-of-level ceiling or base molding line.

Accessories and Furniture

You can stencil lamps, pillows, boxes, bed linens and furniture with borders or elements within each design. One stencil can become a very versatile tool to quickly coordinate an entire room.

Two stencil borders were combined to create this chair rail border.

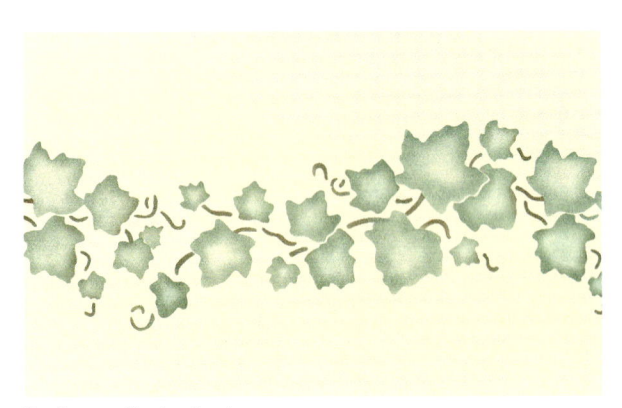

Continuous flowing border.

Straight border.

STENCILING

style options

Vertical Border

A border can be used vertically for a striped effect, or it can be used as an accent around doors and windows. Some designs are not suitable for both vertical and horizontal use—for example, a design with a heart shape element that must be viewed horizontally.

Free-Form

Borders don't have to follow straight lines; they can be used to accent architectural features in the rooms, or they can fall out of corners and drape around doors and windows. Some stencils include additional design motifs, called random elements, which can be used to break up repeats of the border design. You also can stencil on the back of the stencil to reverse the direction of a border design. Just remember to reverse all the overlays.

Design elements can be scattered throughout the wall area to give a hand painted look.

Vertical border.

Random elements combined to create a free-form.

DECORATIVE FINISHES | 39

STENCILING

walls

Surface Preparation

For plaster and drywall surfaces, minimal preparation is required to prepare the wall for stenciling. Review the "Surface Preparation" section on page 15 and consider these additional guidelines:

1. Stenciling can be applied over oil or latex base paints. A quality satin or eggshell finish is recommended. Flat, eggshell or low luster sheens work best with Dry Brush or CreamStix paints. Stencil Gels and acrylics can be used on all paint finishes, including semi-gloss. If stenciling on high-gloss paints, test the paint first for surface curability.
2. Seal the wall with a quality water-base primer if the paint is peeling or chalking. If the stencil paint seems to "sink" into the wall surface (a common problem in older homes or on walls with a poor quality paint), check with your local paint store for a primer that is compatible with the wall paint selected.
3. Stenciling adds an interesting decorator touch over existing wallpaper. If you try to remove the paper and discover that you're also removing the surface of the drywall, leave the wallpaper in place and paint over it with oil-based paint. This is sometimes more practical than removing the paper, resurfacing the wall, sanding and sealing, priming and painting.

Once you have selected the design, made your practice print to determine color and placement, and prepared your wall—it is time to begin stenciling!

Measure and Mark
(Photo A)

Any horizontal or vertical lines that are not directly at the ceiling line or following trim moldings must be plumb to look right—even if the ceiling, floors, or trim moldings are out of plumb. With a light chalk pencil, measure and mark the area where chair rail, dropped border, or vertical border will be placed. Use a bubble or spirit level to align, measure, and mark wall with a broken line. The marks will be erased before or after stenciling. You can also mark vertical lines with a plumb bob and light chalk line.

Position Stencil
(Photo B)

Align the horizontal center markings on the stencil with the line you've marked on the wall. Tape the stencil in place, and you're ready to begin.

When stenciling an entire room, follow this sequence of application:
1. Stencil all horizontals first.
2. Next, add verticals. All vertical lines should be stopped by a horizontal. When stenciling around a door or window, first stencil above the door or window, then stencil the sides down to the char rail or base trim moldings.
3. Add free form or random elements, using stenciled paper proofs to help determine the best placement.

40 DECORATIVE FINISHES

Stenciling into Corners
(Photo A)
1. When you reach the corner with a border, tape the adjacent wall with low-tack masking tape or painter's tape. Wrap the flexible stencil material into the corner. Tape the stencil to the corner of the wall you are stenciling.
2. Tape the top of the stencil portion that falls on the adjacent wall, letting the bottom hang freely.
3. Feather a very dry paint into the corner, actually fading out the print into the corner. Use a light, sweeping stroke.
4. Remove the tape and place it over the area just stenciled. Secure the stencil to the adjacent wall.
5. Feather the paint into the corner so the print is lighter in the corner. A too-dark print will draw the eye to the corner rather than diminish the corner placement.

Taping Off Design Elements
(Photo B)
On some multi-part stencil designs, it is possible to create a different or coordinating design by taping off elements in one or more overlays. Use painter's tape to cover the elements in the design you do not want stenciled.

Stretching or Squeezing a Border Design
Stretching a design involves adding 1/4" to 1/2" to a repeat so a design fits more accurately into a corner or a particular space. Adding more space between the elements within each repeat is the easiest way to stretch; however, if it is a continuous flowing border, the added space can be added with each repeat.

Regular stencil border design using all elements.

Example of taping off design elements.

STENCILING

planning borders

There are two techniques for stenciling borders—continuous and centered. The technique you choose will depend upon the size of the room, the length of the border repeat, and the size of the design elements within the border.

The design layout depends upon the size of the stencil's design repeat. If the stencil repeat is 8" or less, follow the instructions for continuous placement. If the design repeat is more than 8", use the instructions for either continuous or centered placement.

Continuous Technique

The continuous technique can be used when the design elements are small and flow in one direction.

1. Start stenciling at the most evident corner of the room—the corner you would first see when entering the room, usually the corner across from the door. Stencil from this corner to both the left and right, working into the adjacent corners. Stop stenciling when you are about two thirds of the way down the wall, and before getting to another corner.
2. The paper proof you stenciled to practice the design will now become an effective measurement tool. Use it as a visual gauge for the placement of the design. To avoid having a major design element fall in the corner, you may need to stretch or squeeze the repeats (see directions for stretching and squeezing on page 41). Adjust the repeat placement as needed into the corner.
3. To finish, use the proof again to gauge the placement of the design as you approach the last corner. Adjust each repeat as needed. Finish the design in the least noticeable corner.

Centered Technique

Use a centered technique when the design elements are large and the room is small or when using design elements in particular areas, such as the corners.

1. Measure the length of each repeat in the design. Most designs have at least two points that can be designated as the center—usually the center of a dominant element or the space between two elements.
2. Locate and mark the center of the most dominant wall (the one most noticeable when entering the room.)
3. To determine the starting point, walk your paper proof from one possible center point to the corner; then try with the other possible center point. Select the starting center point based on how the design fits into the corner. (By starting at a center of the design and the center of the room, both corners will finish the same.)
4. Continue around the room, stretching or squeezing the repeats as needed, ending in the least conspicuous corner of the room.

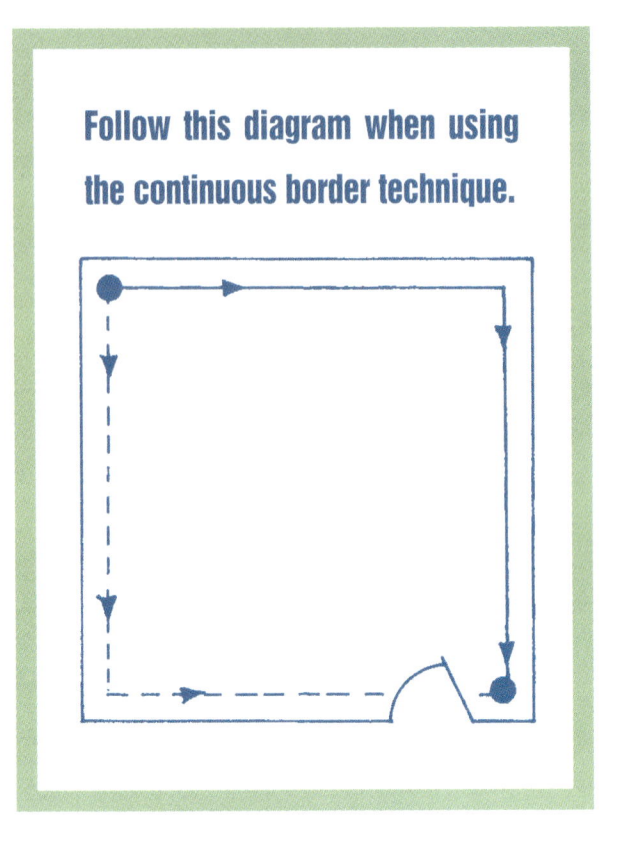

Follow this diagram when using the continuous border technique.

STENCILING

planning borders (continued)

Stenciling Borders with Corner Elements
Stencil the corner elements first. Find the center of each wall and mark with a chalk pencil. Find the center of the border and place it at the center of the wall. Stencil into each corner. Repeat the same procedure on the remaining walls.

Stenciling Spot Motifs or Random Elements
To place spot motifs and free-form elements, stencil several proofs and decide the most effective design placement via positioning of the proofs. For elements that have a definite vertical and horizontal placement, measure and mark the centers of the wall. Check placement with a bubble or spirit level. For motifs such as faux window panes, frames, plates, or shelves, be sure the top edge of the motif is perfectly plumb.

DECORATIVE FINISHES

STENCILING

backgrounds

A background color or texture can have a dramatic effect on your stencil print. The same stencil can take on a completely different look when applied to different background colors. When working with background colors, be sure to paint the paper proof with the background color so you can test the intensity of the design.

Stenciling on Dark Backgrounds

Dark colors can be dramatic backgrounds for stenciling. In order to get more contrast, first stencil the design in white acrylic paint and let dry. Stencil over the white design in the colors of your choice. This method is particularly effective in enhancing the look of translucent stencil gels.

Creating a Glazed Background

An affordable alternative to repainting a smudged or "tired" wall is to basecoat the wall with a translucent glaze color.

Once the wall surface is glazed, a stamp is pressed against the wet glaze to create a negative, or relief, print. The stencil is then applied very lightly with a roller.

For further information and ideas for creating backgrounds on walls and other surfaces, see the Faux Finishing section (page 61).

Composite Design

Elements from several stencils can be combined to create a new stencil design. This technique is especially effective if adding a motif to a surface band painted a different color than the wall surface. When combining stencils, work first on paper proofs, then tape the proof to the wall area to see if the elements are balanced and coordinated.

Stenciling on dark backgrounds.

Glazed background.

This design was created with three stencils.

DECORATIVE FINISHES

STENCILING

backgrounds (continued)

Examples of a design stenciled on different background colors.

STENCILING

special effects

Shading
(Photo A)

Shading adds depth and dimension within a stencil print. For example, shading can be used to add feathered wings to a bird or folds within a leaf. Create a template by cutting a shape from an index card or freezer paper, use the dropout piece from the stencil, or an edge of the stencil itself.

1. Hold the template on the completed stencil print and position the brush so most of the bristles are on the template and just a few are on the cutout area. Stencil the area with a light circular stroke, stroking in the same direction across the entire area.
2. Dry Brush paint or CreamStix work exceptionally well for this technique because the color can be softened or lightly smudged with a paper towel or your finger.

Tone-on-Tone

The tranquility of tone-on-tone color is easy to achieve with stenciling. Simply use the same stenciling color for all the overlays. Subtle variations in the tone-on-tone look can be achieved by varying the pressure and paint application technique when using either a brush or roller. Decorator Glaze is an ideal choice for tone-on-tone stenciling—the translucent color blends naturally, and the longer "open" (wet) time allows the colors to be manipulated for a sheer print with a shaded edge.

The tone-on-tone technique gives a soft, understated look.

Example of template shading.

Another example of template shading.

46 | DECORATIVE FINISHES

STENCILING

special effects (continued)

Shadows can be used to create depth and volume in stenciled motifs. An object that casts a shadow appears to have form and mass; thus shadows are added to stenciled motifs to enhance their realism and clarify their presence within a space. Depending on where and how it is used, a stenciled shadow should take into account the direction, quality and quantity of the existing light source so that it doesn't conflict visually with natural shadows. Also, shadows or motifs that are adjacent to each other should cast shadows of similar quality and length.

To create shadows, use the dropout or cutout portion of the stencil, if available, as a template to mask the stenciled design and to create subtle shaded contours. Shadows can also be added freehand as a detail or finishing touch.

Drop Shadow
1. After stenciling the design, move the stencil slightly to the right and down. Stencil a second print with a very light application of the same color. **(Photo A)**
2. The letter appears to be sitting several inches in front of the wall, with the shadow being cast by the letter. **(Photo B)**

Freehand Shadow
(Photo C)
Another method of adding shadows is to add a light gray or umber shadow on two sides of the print. If there is no "natural" light source, you can create one but must keep that source consistent with all shadows.

Mix dark paint with water to an inky consistency. Test the color and pigmentation on a sample print. If not dark enough, add more paint. If too dark, add more water. Load a flat brush with the thinned paint and blot on paper towel. Add shadow to the stencil print, following the outline of the print on the side opposite the real or imagined light source.

Shadowing with a Stencil Overlay
Some stencils have a shadow stencil as part of the design. Align the shadow stencil opposite the light source and stencil lightly using a small, very dry brush.

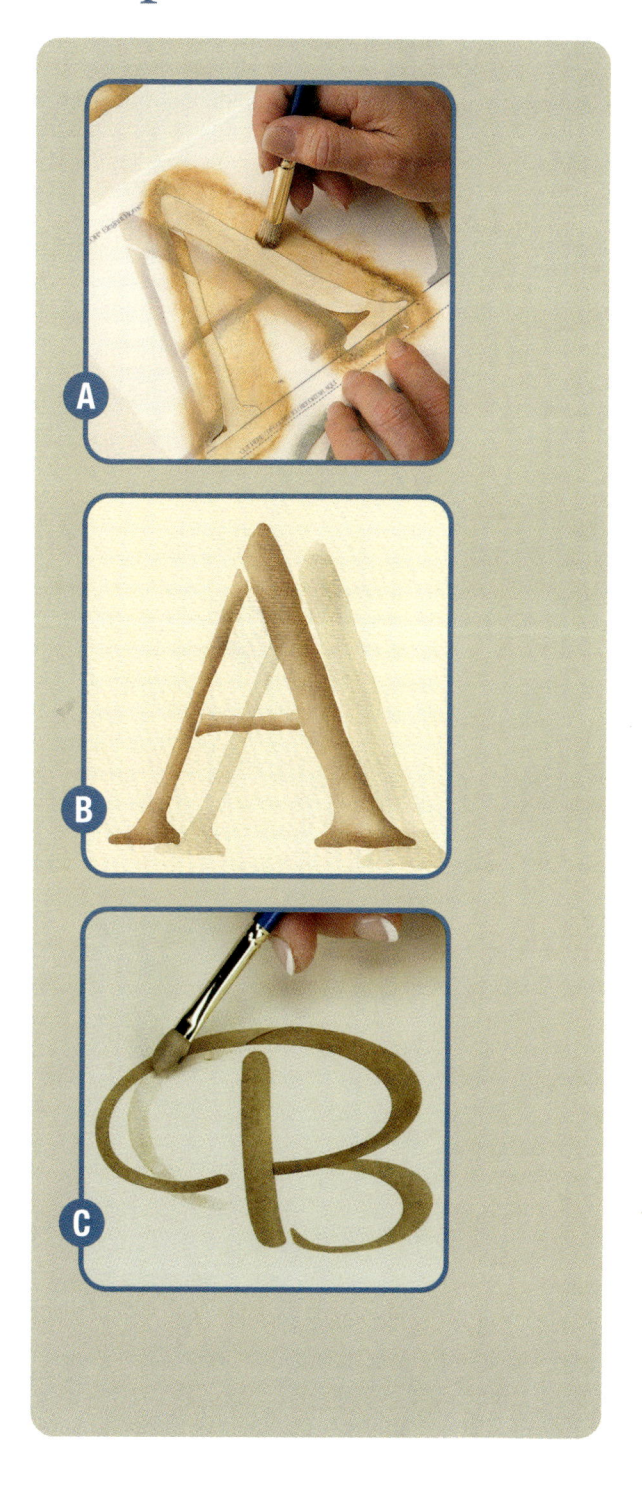

DECORATIVE FINISHES | **47**

STENCILING

wood surfaces

Paneled Walls

1. Preparation: On unfinished wood or plywood paneling, apply a base stain or clear wood sealer. Let dry, following manufacturer's instructions. On pre-finished paneling, wash to remove wax and/or dirt, then prime before painting.
2. Stain, paint, or glaze to create the background desired.
3. Stencil as you would on any wall surface.
4. Based on the washability required, apply a waterbased top coat (see Finishing Wood, pg.49).

Stained Backgrounds or Raw Wood Surfaces

1. Sand wood with fine sandpaper. Always sand with the grain of the wood. Wipe clean with a tack cloth.
2. Seal with a clear wood sealer before staining unless the stain you're using already contains a sealer. Let surface dry.
3. Test the stain on the inside of a drawer, the underside of a chair, or on a scrap piece of wood to see how the surface will accept the stain. Let dry. If the test is to your liking, apply stain according to manufacturer's instructions. Let dry.
4. If the wood is very porous, apply a thin coat of a spray matte sealer to the stained surface so any mistakes you might make when stenciling can be easily removed.
5. Stencil following basic stenciling instructions for the type of paint you are using. Let stencil paint dry.
6. Apply a finish coat (see Finishing Wood, pg. 49).

Example of stenciling on exterior siding.

Example of stenciling on stained wood.

DECORATIVE FINISHES

STENCILING

wood surfaces (continued)

Painted Backgrounds or Raw Wood
1. Sand wood with fine sandpaper. Always sand with the grain of the wood. Wipe clean with tack cloth.
2. Optional: Prime with a primer suitable for wood. If wood has knotholes, the areas around these knotholes, especially in pine, will bleed through the paint if not properly sealed. On cedar and pine, use a quick-drying primer specifically recommended by your local paint dealer. Sand the surface lightly before applying the basecoat.
3. Basecoat with 2-3 coats water based paint. Let dry and sand between coats.
4. Stencil and let stencil paint dry thoroughly.
5. Apply a finish coat (see Finishing Wood, below).

Glossy Surfaces—such as painted or finished furniture
1. Clean surface thoroughly and wipe with a tack cloth.
2. Lightly sand surface or buff with #0000 steel wool to give a slight tooth to the surface sheen.
3. Stencil with acrylic colors or stencil gel. Use a brush, roller, or sponge applicator. Shade with a darker color. Allow paints to cure for 72 hours.
4. Mist with a clear matte acrylic sealer.
5. On some surfaces, such as kitchen cabinets, protect the entire surface with a water based finish, such as polyacrylic.

Finishing Wood
Waterbased finishes can be used for both interior and exterior surfaces. When using a waterbase finish over an acrylic or water based stencil paint, it may be necessary to seal the stencil paint first by lightly misting with an acrylic spray sealer. Do not heavily brush over the acrylic paint as it could begin to run, depending on the base surface. When in doubt, always mist first with a clear sealer!

1. Work in an area where dust is at a minimum and remove hairs or specks of dirt if you see them on the surface.
2. Using a quality brush or applicator, apply the first coat with the grain of the wood, following manufacturer's instructions. Use a round china bristle brush to apply finish to pieces that aren't flat, such as chair legs or spindles. Let dry.
3. Be sure the finish does not run or puddle—several light coats are better than one heavy coat—and allow adequate drying time between coats.
4. Wipe the entire piece with a tack cloth, and apply a second coat. Let dry.
5. Buff surface with a piece of crumpled brown paper bag. For a hand-rubbed look, lightly sprinkle surface with water and sand very lightly with #600 wet/dry sandpaper. Wipe entire piece with a tack cloth to remove dust and excess water.
6. Apply 2-4 more coats. Let dry and wipe with a tack cloth between coats.
7. Lightly buff with #0000 steel wool. Optional: Apply a coat of wax designed for furniture. Wipe off all residue with a tack cloth.

DECORATIVE FINISHES

STENCILING

floorcloths, rugs and floors

Floors, floorcloths and woven rugs provide wonderful opportunities to decorate with stenciling.

Canvas Floorcloths

Traditional floorcloths are made of a heavy #10 weight unprimed canvas. Floorcloth canvas can be purchased in pre-cut sizes and rolls. The canvas has been treated with gesso and is ready to stencil if you want a white background. If using raw canvas, it must be stretched and painted with gesso before beginning or the floorcloth will buckle.

Vinyl Floorcloths

Vinyl flooring is readily accessible and very affordable. Remnant pieces are available at home center stores or flooring companies. The pieces can be cut to any size or dimension and offer a non-skid, protective surface for the flooring underneath. Select a remnant without an adhesive back or a smooth, shiny vinyl backing.

1. Prime the back with bonder/primer/sealer and let dry.
2. Paint with latex wall paint in the color of your choice.
3. Treat the surface as if it were a wall. Add faux backgrounds, striping or borders. For stripes, use low tack masking tape to mask off so that the base color will not be removed.
4. Stencil the surface and let area cure for 3-4 days.
5. Apply 3-5 coats of a waterbase topcoat, such as a satin finish polyacrylic. The finish will dry hard and will not amber or discolor.
6. Lightly buff the dried surface with crumpled pieces of a paper bag after the final coat.
7. To clean, wipe with a damp cloth. If the floorcloth begins to show wear, clean surface and apply additional coats of topcoat.

50 | DECORATIVE FINISHES

STENCILING

floorcloths, rugs and floors (continued)

Woven Rugs

Tightly woven cotton throw rugs, rag rugs, and sisal or straw rugs can also be stenciled. The rug provides background texture and color. Inexpensive rugs are available at discount, import and outlet stores.

1. Lay rug flat. Stencil with either stencil gels or acrylic paints. For maximum colorfastness, mix a few drops of textile medium into the brush when loading into the paint.
2. If the rug has a high nap, use a pouncing stroke to apply paint. Apply paint generously in several light coats. Shading should be done with a darker color paint rather than a lighter or heavier application stroke.
3. Allow rug to dry thoroughly 24-36 hours before folding. If possible, heat set by tumbling in a hot dryer for 30-45 minutes. If the rug is sisal, or too large for the dryer, heat set with an iron, following basic instructions for fabric stenciling (see page 52).

Floors

1. Before stenciling an unvarnished wood floor, remove dirt and wax and seal with a clear sealer or a penetrating stain to protect the wood and allow for even paint distribution.
2. For a pre-finished or glossy wood floor, remove all dirt and wax. Lightly sand.
3. Stencil the floor as desired and let cure.
4. Consult your local paint store for the appropriate top coat. Waterbased finishes are extremely durable, easy to apply, low in odor and fast drying, when compared to oil based finishes. Walk gently on the surface of an unsealed floor, or cover with cotton rugs until the finish can be applied.

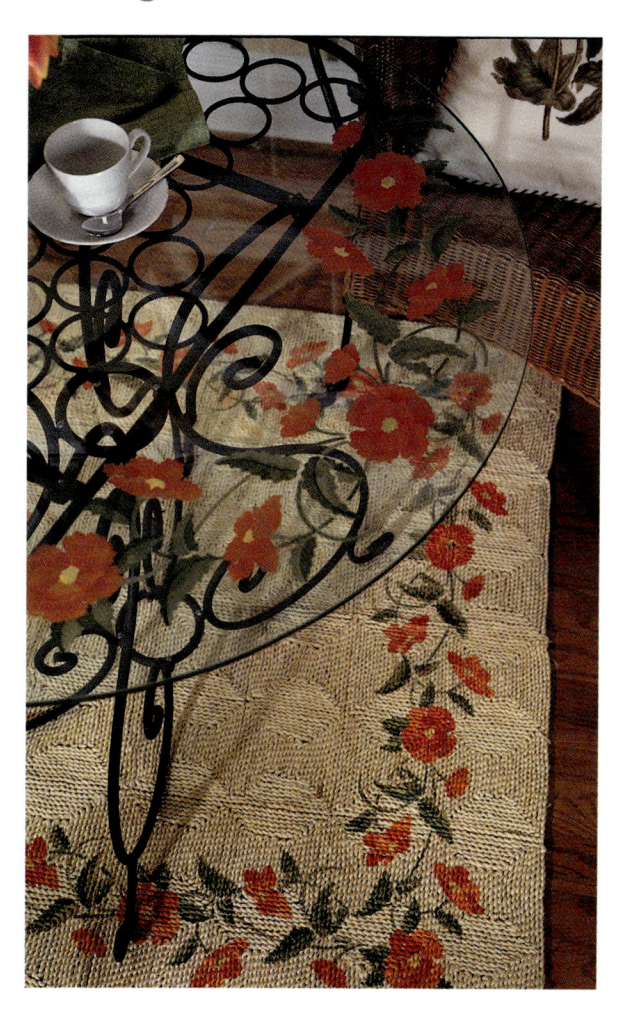

DECORATIVE FINISHES | 51

STENCILING

fabric surfaces

Use stenciling to give a custom look to sheets, tablecloths, clothing, tote bags and more.

Stenciling on Fabric

1. All fabrics should be pre-washed to remove sizing prior to painting.
2. To keep fabric from moving, insert a piece of fine sandpaper underneath the fabric. **(Photo A)**
3. Position the stencil on the fabric and tape securely in place. **(Photo B)**
4. Load the brush and lightly pounce on a paper towel to offload excess paint. Begin on an uncut part of the stencil and bring the paint into the cutout area using a very light stroke. Shade the outside edge of the design with a heavier stroke or with a darker tone of paint. **(Photo C)**

Heat Setting

1. After the project has dried, set an iron on the "wool" settting. Do not use steam. Place a scrap of muslin, a pressing cloth or linen towel over the stenciled print.
2. Working in sections, press the design with the iron for approximately 30 seconds. Rotate the iron slowly over the fabric so that the heat is evenly distributed.
3. Repeat on the wrong side of the fabric.

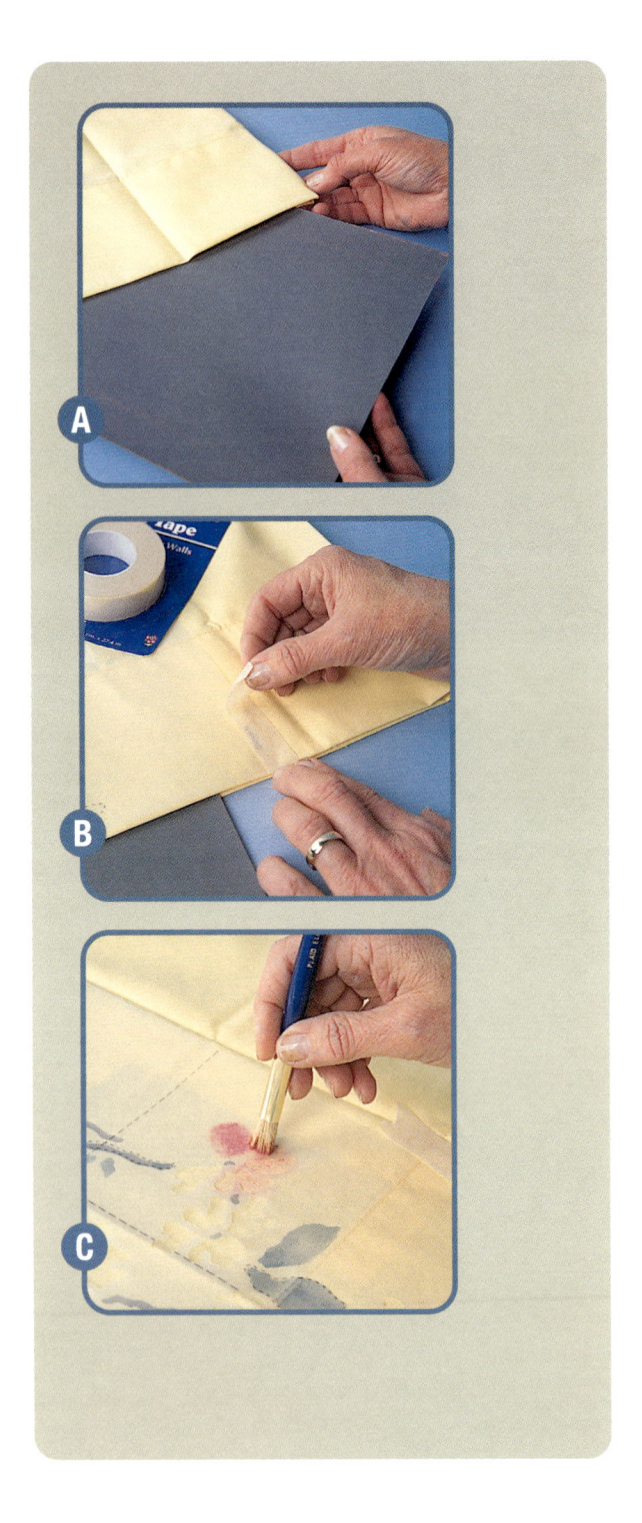

HELPFUL HINTS:

- Liquid or Dry Brush paints can be used on fabrics. When using acrylic paint, mix with Textile Medium before stenciling.
- Neatness is important; it is difficult to remove mistakes from fabric. Remove smudges immediately with a stencil eraser or paint remover (test fabric before applying).
- Work paint thoroughly into fibers for maximum colorfastness.
- Insert a piece of cardboard between layers of fabric to keep paint from bleeding through. For thin fabrics, place a paper towel or plain paper under the fabric.
- Plan your design with paper proofs.
- When stenciling on dark fabrics, stencil an undercoat design in white paint or stencil gel. Let dry and stencil in the desired color over the undercoat.

52 DECORATIVE FINISHES

STENCILING

fabric surfaces (continued)

STENCILING

embossing

Embossing is a technique that creates a raised design on a paper surface, such as a greeting card or memory album. Embossing is done with a stylus that has a smooth metal ball tip. Select a stylus size that will fit into the openings of the stencil.

Embossing Technique

1. Working on a light table or at a window on a sunny day, tape a piece of paper facedown on a stencil. Use the tip of the stylus to gently trace around the edge of the stencil design. **(Photo A)** Apply enough pressure to push the paper into the stencil—but not so much that you tear the paper. Lift the paper and turn over to reveal the embossed or raised surface.
2. To add color to the embossed design, place the embossed paper, right side up, on a flat surface. Tape the stencil in place, wrong side up, aligning the design with the embossed surface. Stencil with a very dry brush using stencil gels or dry brush paint. **(Photo B)**

DECORATIVE FINISHES

STENCILING

aging stencil prints

A stencil print can be made to look as if has weathered the test of time. Naturally, this type of print would not have crisp edges and would have a diffused or worn look. You can recreate this aged look by using a few simple techniques.

Aging Technique

1. Paint surface with the background color desired and let dry. To get a streaked or washed look, thin paint with water so that an even coverage is not achieved. When dry, lightly sand with fine grit sanding block to remove some of the paint. Remove small areas of paint so that bare wood or wall surface shows through.
2. Stencil with a light pouncing stroke using a very dry brush with Stencil Gel or Decorator Glaze. Stencil into the center of the cut out area and very lightly pounce out to the edge of the design.
3. Before stencil paint dries, lift stencil and lightly pounce or sweep edge of print, diffusing or blurring the edge.
4. Once paint has dried, lightly sand surface with a fine sanding block, using a light sweeping motion and working in the same direction as before. This will give a rubbed look to the stencil print. Stop sanding when you have achieved a look you like.

DECORATIVE FINISHES

STENCILING

colorways

56 DECORATIVE FINISHES

STENCILING

colorways (continued)

DECORATIVE FINISHES   57

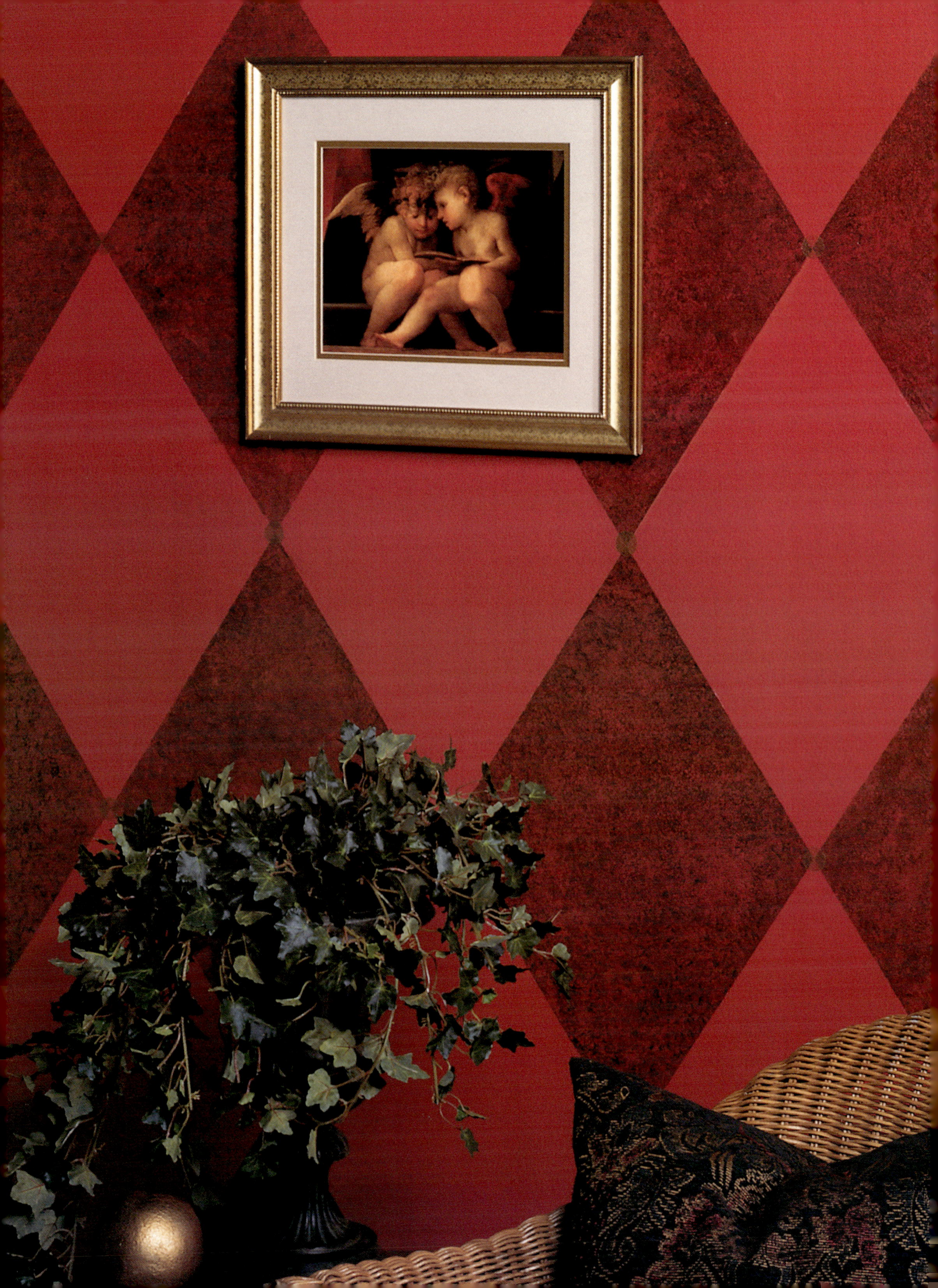

FAUX FINISHING

Faux finishing is an exciting alternative to plain paint or wallpaper. The term encompasses a variety of finishes created with special glazes and tools, including sponging, ragging, mopping, combing, antiquing, marbling, and more. The right combination of technique and color can transform a room, adding interest and a touch of elegance.

This section of Decorative Finishes will take you, step-by-step, through the many styles and applications of faux finishing. Be sure to review the information on design and color at the beginning of the book – let it be your guide as you plan the finish for your room or accessory piece.

Faux finishing is easy and enjoyable! Once you become familiar with a few basic techniques, you'll be able to create professional-looking results anywhere in your home.

FAUX FINISHING

tools and materials

The increasing popularity of faux finishing makes it easy to find tools and materials at nearly any craft, hardware, or home improvement store. Listed below are the basic tools you'll need, depending on which type of finish you choose.

Decorator Mitts
Decorator mitts consist of a specialized fabric or sponge pad attached to pocket that is worn on the hand. The mitts are dipped into glaze and applied to the surface to create textures such as ragging, sponging, or mopping. They can also be used to remove glaze from a wall to create a reverse finished effect.

Decorator Tools
Essential to the faux finisher, decorator tools consist of combs and brushes in a variety of sizes and styles, wood-graining tools, sponges, and stipplers. These hand-held tools are pulled or brushed over wet glaze to create stripes, fabric effects, crackle finishes, clouds, wood grain, and more.

Decorator Glazes
This translucent, slow-drying medium is specially formulated to provide subtle color and dramatic results in faux finishing. Glaze can be used alone over existing wall or surface color, as a base color accented with a complimentary faux finish, or combined for stunning results. (See page 14 for details on glazes.)

Additional Tools and Materials
Paper or foam plates for a disposable and readily accessible palette
Cardboard scraps for blotting mitts and offloading glaze
Chalk pencil for marking walls
Plumb line
Masking tape
Ladder

60 | DECORATIVE FINISHES

FAUX FINISHING

general instructions

Mixing Glaze
Faux finishes are created with a mixture of Neutral Decorator Glaze and Decorator Glaze color. Mix equal amounts or three parts Neutral to one part color. **(Photo A)** See label and individual technique instructions for recommended proportions. Neutral glazes can also be combined with any latex paint.

Mix the appropriate amount for the job. Disposable plates can be used for small amounts. For walls, pour color directly into the Neutral Glaze tub. **(Photo B)**

Surface Preparation
Surfaces should be clean, smooth, and free of dust and grease. Wood surfaces should be sanded smooth and wiped with a tack cloth. Patch holes and cracks with a patching compound appropriate to the wall and sand smooth. Be sure to wear a dust mask or respirator when sanding and vacuuming up sanding dust.

Base Painting
Base coat the surface with 1-3 coats of paint. Let dry, sanding between coats with 220 grit sandpaper if painting wood. On walls, use a satin or eggshell finish.

Masking Off
Mask off any areas of a room that are not to be glazed with low-tack masking tape. Use a "long mask" on surfaces where you'll be leaving the tape for more than one day (moldings, ceiling lines, etc.). For areas where tape will be removed within hours, use "easy mask" tape, which won't damage base paint or previously glazed areas.

Practice Boards
Create a practice board to check the color and to become familiar with the techniuqe. Use poster board, wood, or gypsum wall board. The light in the room is one determining factor for how intense or vivid a finish should be. In dim light, more contrast will be more pleasing. In brighter settings, more sedate and mellow finishes are appropriate. Place the finished practice board in the room and observe. If the glaze appears too intense, add more Neutral to the mixture. If it looks too pale, add more colored Decorator Glaze.

Working in Corners
Tape the adjacent wall with low-tack masking tape and work the mitt or tool into the corner. The tape keeps the adjacent wall from getting smeared. Remove tape and let dry completely. Tape on the other side and continue.

Finishing
On glazed walls, sealing is not necessary. Once the glaze has dried 24-48 hours, it is cured and durable enough to wipe with a damp cloth. Glazed woodwork should be sealed to protect the surface. Choose a product compatible with acrylic paints.

DECORATIVE FINISHES

FAUX FINISHING

ragging

Ragging is an easy-to-achieve finish that uses the texture of cloth to create a pattern. The effects can be subtle or dramatic, depending on the contrast between the colors used.

Ragging Technique

1. Dip the face of the ragging mitt in water, wring out, and pat on a towel. Pour a small amount of prepared glaze onto a disposable plate. With the mitt on your hand, press the face of the mitt into the glaze. **(Photo A)** Pounce the mitt on a piece of cardboard to offload excess glaze.
2. Pat the wall randomly and repeatedly with the mitt, overlapping to achieve consistent coverage. **(Photo B)** Change hand position frequently. Rinse and reload the mitt as necessary.

Ragging in Corners

To work in corners, tape off the adjacent wall to prevent smearing. Place the mitt at the corner and use your free hand to press it against the wall. Repeat until the corner is complete. Work the corners at the same time you're working on adjacent walls so that the color and texture will be consistent with the walls.

Ragging can be achieved using wadded-up rags; however, a ragging mitt makes the technique much easier.

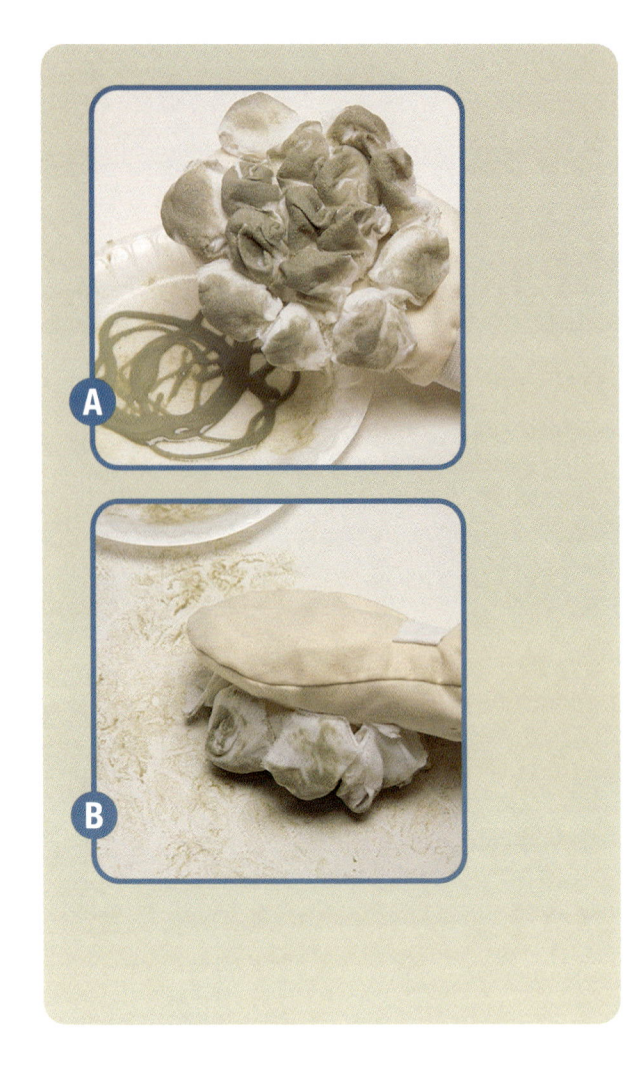

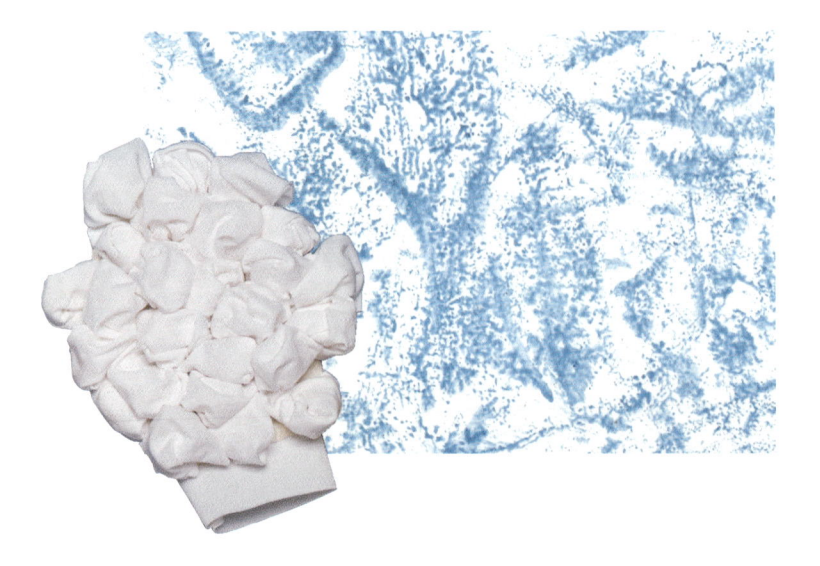

62 DECORATIVE FINISHES

FAUX FINISHING

ragging (continued)

To create ragged stripes, use a plumb line to mark a straight vertical line on the wall in pencil. Mark stripes at desired intervals with masking tape and apply color with the ragging mitt (you will be ragging every other stripe). Remove tape and let the color dry. Apply tape to mark the remaining stripes and apply color with the ragging mitt.

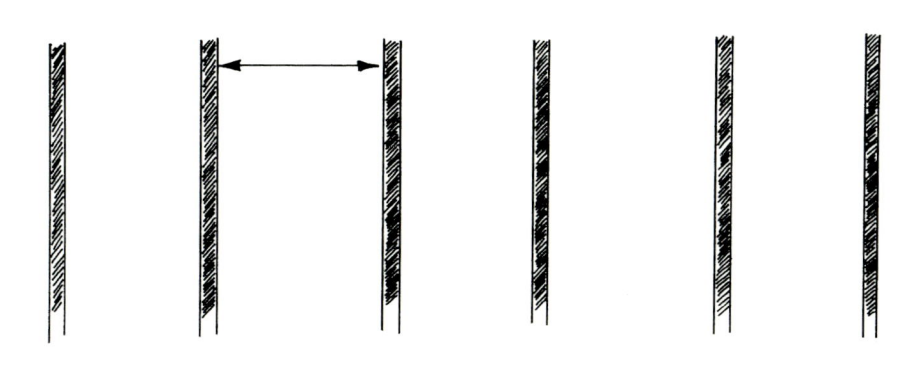

DECORATIVE FINISHES | 63

FAUX FINISHING

sponging

Sponging is a time-honored technique that uses a sponge to create texture. Sponging can be as simple as a single color on top of a base coat, or layers of color can be added to create more interest and texture. Hand-painting or stenciling the surface, either before or after sponging, can enhance the look.

Sponging Technique
1. Moisten the sponge with water to make it soft and pliable. Wring to remove excess water. Pour a small amount of prepared glaze onto a disposable plate. Press the sponge into the glaze and blot on a piece of cardboard to offload excess glaze. **(Photo A)**
2. Press the sponge to the wall unevenly and randomly. **(Photo B)** Some areas should cover the wall solidly, while in others, the base color should show through. Rinse and reload the sponge as necessary.

Almost any type of sponge can be used: natural ocean sponge, household cellulose sponge, or a Sponging Mitt. If using a household cellulose sponge, pinch off the straight edge for a natural look.

HELPFUL HINTS:
- Don't press too hard or move the sponge on the surface—you'll create smears. Simply press directly on the surface, pull away, and press again.

- Each time the sponge is lifted from the surface, change the position of the sponge and press it near or slightly on top of the previous sponged area. This prevents a repeat pattern.

- Using a sponge to smear, pat, and rub the surface is called "scumbling." It's a softer, looser more subtle look.

- If the wrist of the Sea Sponging Mitt is too large for you, use a rubber band or masking tape to secure it.

64 DECORATIVE FINISHES

FAUX FINISHING

sponging (continued)

To create this striking room, basecoat walls in cream. Mark stripes with masking tape and paint in tan. Once dry, sponge the entire area with a mixture of Neutral and gold glazes.

DECORATIVE FINISHES | **65**

FAUX FINISHING

mopping

The mopping technique is very similar to that of sponging or ragging, but the texture created is much different. A Mopping Mitt, which has tightly woven loops of strings, makes the process easy.

Mopping Technique

To create a mopped finish, follow the instructions for ragging on page 62.

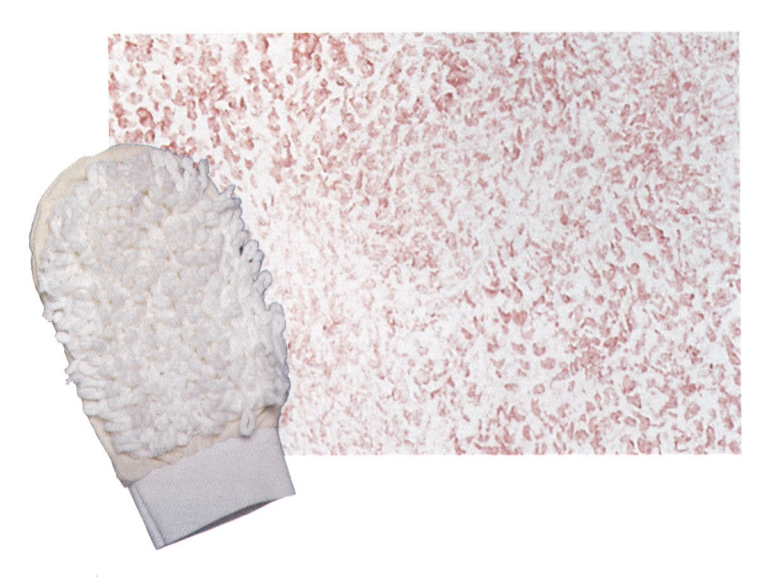

FAUX FINISHING

french brush

The fine, short bristles of a French Brush can be used to create a variety of unique decorative finishes. The brush can be used to apply color (positive application) or to remove color (negative application). Color can be stippled or brushed to create a variety of interesting looks.

Positive Application Technique

1. Place a small amount of prepared glaze on a disposable plate. Dip the tips of the bristles in the glaze. Pounce the brush on a disposable plate to work the paint into the bristles. **(Photo A)**
2. Hold the brush perpendicular to the wall and pounce the brush on the surface, pressing hard enough to force the bristles apart. **(Photo B)** Repeat until wall has been covered.

DECORATIVE FINISHES | **67**

FAUX FINISHING

french brush (continued)

Negative Application Technique
1. Working in small sections, apply glaze to the wall surface with a roller or sponge brush. **(Photo A)**
2. While the glaze is still wet, stroke with the French Brush to remove glaze and create texture. **(Photo B)** Periodically wipe the bristles of the brush with a damp rag to remove glaze buildup.

French Brushed walls using two coordinating glaze colors.

A

B

HELPFUL HINT:
When stippling in more than one color, you may find it helpful to use two brushes. Be sure to wipe the bristles frequently to prevent the colors from building up and turning muddy.

DECORATIVE FINISHES

FAUX FINISHING

french brush (continued)

The French Brush can be used with a stippling technique to create the airy look of clouds and sky.

Creating Faux Sky

1. To create this look, start with a pale blue ceiling. Mix equal parts neutral glaze and white paint. In separate containers, mix soft yellow and light pink paint with equal amounts of neutral glaze.
2. Dip the tips of the French Brush bristles into the white glaze mixture. Pounce the brush on a disposable plate to work the paint into the bristles.
3. Pounce onto the ceiling to create drifts of soft white clouds. Periodically wipe the brush with a damp rag to prevent glaze buildup; reload as needed.
4. Use the edge of the brush to work in small amounts of yellow and pink paint to create shadows and shading at the edge of the clouds.

DECORATIVE FINISHES | 69

FAUX FINISHING

stippler brush

The Stippler Brush is a wonderful tool for creating interesting faux effects. The brush can be used for positive and negative application. In a positive application, the glaze is applied to the surface with the brush; for negative application, the brush is used to remove glaze from the surface.

Positive Application Technique
(Photo A)
1. Place a small amount of prepared glaze on a disposable plate. Dip the tips of the bristles in the glaze. Pounce the brush on a disposable plate to work the paint into the bristles.
2. Hold the brush perpendicular to the wall and pounce the brush on the surface, pressing hard enough to force the bristles apart. Repeat until wall has been covered.

Negative Application Technique
(Photo B)
1. Working in small sections, apply glaze to the wall with a roller or sponge brush.
2. While the glaze is still wet, stroke with the Stippler Brush to remove glaze and create texture. Periodically wipe the bristles of the brush with a damp rag to remove glaze buildup.

Positive application

Negative application

70 | DECORATIVE FINISHES

FAUX FINISHING

stippler brush (continued)

These walls were finished using the positive application technique.

DECORATIVE FINISHES | 71

FAUX FINISHING

wall weaver

It's easy to create the look of linen or chambray fabric with a wall weaver brush. In this technique, the brush is simply pulled through wet glaze – first vertically, then horizontally.

Wall Weaver Technique
1. Working in sections, use a foam brush or paint roller to apply glaze to the painted surface.
2. Pull the wall weaver brush across the surface using long, straight strokes in one direction, cutting through the glaze with the bristles. **(Photo A)** Repeat this step, pulling the brush perpendicular to the first strokes to create a woven fabric effect. **(Photo B)**
3. Completed woven effect.

HELPFUL HINTS:
- The more you pull the brush through the glaze, the lighter the glaze color will become because you are removing glaze from the surface with each pull of the brush.
- Keep a soft, moist cloth handy for wiping the bristles occasionally to remove glaze buildup.
- Do not rinse the brush until you are finished and do not use a brush that has been freshly cleaned with water, even if it feels dry. The moisture in the bristles will dilute the glaze and can cause drips and runs. To clean the brush, wash with water and Brush Plus® Brush Cleaner. Towel dry the bristles and allow to air dry flat so water can drain from the bristles. Let dry 12-24 hours.

DECORATIVE FINISHES

FAUX FINISHING

wall weaver (continued)

These walls were finished using the Wall Weaver brush to create faux denim fabric.

DECORATIVE FINISHES

FAUX FINISHING

combing

An amazing variety of patterns can be created with a combing tool – stripes, weaves, stone, crosshatching, and more. The Standard and Multi-Purpose combing tools have three combing edges for a multitude of effects.

Negative Application Technique
When combing, use a negative application technique – brush or roll glaze onto the surface, then pull the comb through it to create texture.

Multi-Purpose Comb Techniques
Bird's Eye edge. **(Photo A)**
Malachite edge. **(Photo B)**
Marquetry edge. **(Photo C)**

Standard comb

Multi-Purpose comb (floater edge)

A

B

C

74 | DECORATIVE FINISHES

FAUX FINISHING

combing (continued)

HELPFUL HINTS:

- The patterns created depend on the movement used when pulling the teeth across the wet glaze—create a straight pattern, wiggles, or curves. You also can comb the surface, allow the glaze to completely dry, roll or brush another coat of glaze onto the surface, and re-comb, creating another pattern.

- Work in a cool area with no air movement—warm temperatures and moving air (from fans or breezes) cause the glaze to dry faster.

- Practice your technique on painted poster board. If you press too hard, the comb will bend and the result will be messy. If you do not press firmly enough, the teeth will not cut through the glaze evenly.

- You can easily work on curved or slanted areas—simply pull the comb over the surface. But don't expect to create straight lines; aim for a carefree, artistic pattern.

This tailored bathroom features neutral tones with a dramatic twist. The lower half of the wall was masked off and painted in a checkerboard pattern. Both the upper and lower sections were glazed and combed.

DECORATIVE FINISHES | 75

FAUX FINISHING

combing (continued)

Combing in Tight Spaces

Be sure to comb the entire wall surface, close to trims and moldings, around vents and outlets. If there are narrow places where the comb won't fit, purchase a second comb and cut it to fit.

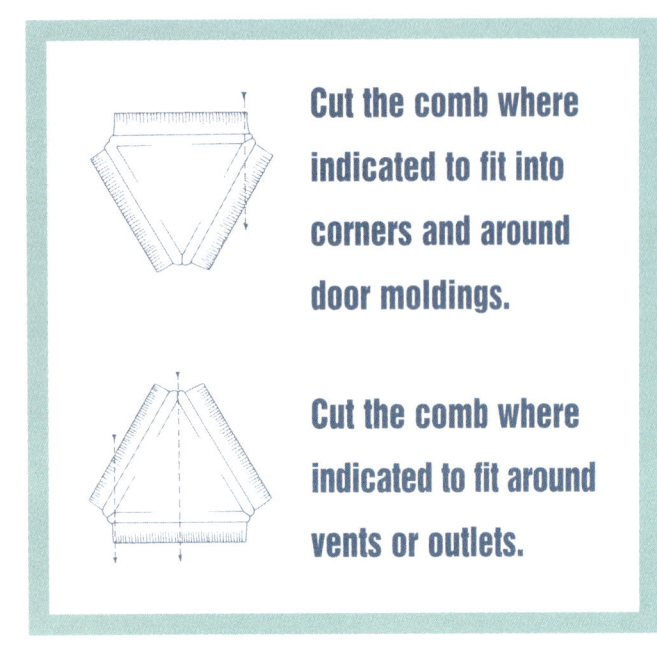

Cut the comb where indicated to fit into corners and around door moldings.

Cut the comb where indicated to fit around vents or outlets.

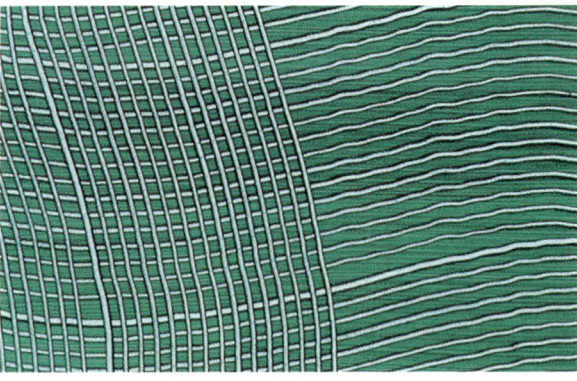

Multi-Purpose comb (bird's eye edge)

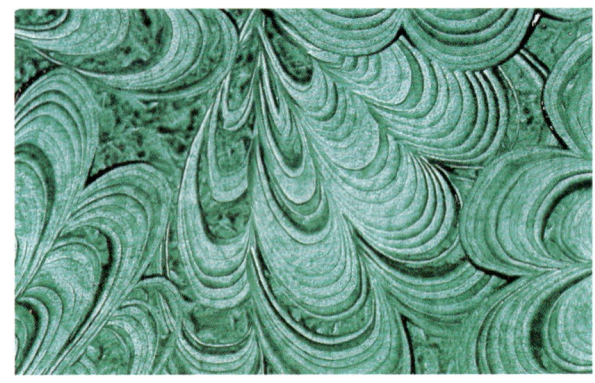

Multi-Purpose comb (malachite edge)

Standard comb (using three edges)

Standard comb (using three edges)

76 | DECORATIVE FINISHES

FAUX FINISHING

spattering

Spattering imparts an aged look to any surface. It's a great finish by itself or in combination with other finishes, such as antiquing or distressing. A one-color spatter adds color and texture; adding two or more colors can achieve a stone effect. Larger spatters give a splashed appearance.

Spattering Technique
(Photo A)
A few drops of water to a teaspoon of acrylic paint. For a more transparent appearance, add Neutral Glaze. Dip the tips of a toothbrush (for smaller projects) or bristle brush in the paint. Run your thumb over the bristles to release the paint, spattering paint specs over the surface.

The top of this interesting table was masked into sections and painted in various pastel shades. Spatters were created using a bristle brush and thinned blue paint. A second spattering of black was then added.

DECORATIVE FINISHES | **77**

FAUX FINISHING

antiquing

Antiquing is a wash of soft-hued color brushed over a surface to impart the appearance of age. Usually, a darker tone is applied over a lighter color. Antiquing creates a subtle patina on the painted surface.

Antiquing Technique

1. Mix Decorator Glaze color with Neutral Glaze to achieve the desired tone. **(Photo A)**
2. Moisten a sponge and squeeze out excess water. Dip one flat surface of the sponge in the glaze mixture. Starting at one edge, lay the sponge on the surface and pull across in long smooth strokes. **(Photo B)** Repeat until the surface is covered.

Light blue basecoat antiqued with dark blue glaze.

Light yellow basecoat antiqued with gold glaze.

> To antique with a brush, dip the tips of the French Brush into the glaze and brush onto the surface using long, smooth strokes.

78 | DECORATIVE FINISHES

FAUX FINISHING

antiquing (continued)

Update a wooden chair with paint and antiquing. The chair was basecoated with a linen-tone paint, then antiqued with a darker glaze color.

FAUX FINISHING

distressing

Distressed finishes look comfortably worn. You can create this look of age and wear by applying wax to some areas of a surface before painting or applying wax between layers of paint. In areas where wax has been applied, the paint is easy to remove.

Distressing Technique

1. Apply wax to surface with the grain of the wood, concentrating the wax in areas where paint would most likely be worn away by handling, such as edges. **(Photo A)** If you're using a base paint, apply 1-3 coats of the base color and let dry, then apply the wax.
2. Apply 1-3 coats of paint. **(Photo B)** The paint coats can be the same color or different colors. Let dry between coats but **do not** sand between coats. Let dry.
3. Scrape surface with a metal scraper edge, working in the direction of the wood grain, to reveal the raw wood or base paint or both. **(Photo C)** In areas where wax was applied, paint will flake off easily. Brush away the paint particles as you scrape.
4. Sand surface to smooth areas where paint has been removed. **(Photo D)**

Other Effects

When working on new wood that you want to give an aged appearance, use a brown antiquing or glaze to rub the exposed wood areas. If the glaze or antiquing discolors the paint, carefully sand the paint to return it to the original color. Another choice is to apply the antiquing to the entire surface—even over the paint—to give it an aged patina.

For a layered effect, use two or more paint colors. Allow paint to dry between colors and rub the wax over the painted surface before adding the next color. When all paint colors are applied and dry and the surface is scraped, the layers of paint will be exposed.

HELPFUL HINTS:

- For surfaces other than wood, or if you don't want the wood to show, base paint the surface, then apply the wax and a second coat of paint. When scraping, you'll expose the first paint color, not the bare wood. This technique can be used to distress terra cotta, plaster, papier mache, gypsum wall board, or concrete.

- Use sanding pads or sandpaper wrapped around a block of wood on flat areas. On curved areas, wrap the sandpaper around your index finger. In tight, straight areas, fold the sandpaper a few times to create a thickness that fits the area.

DECORATIVE FINISHES

FAUX FINISHING

distressing (continued)

Distressed furniture doesn't need a protective finish; after all, if it becomes more distressed, it should not matter. But you may choose to seal tabletops from ring marks or food stains with matte varnish. Don't use satin or gloss varnish—it would impart a sheen that's out of character with a distressed look.

The painted finish of this classic bed style has been lightly sanded to give it a patina that only loving use usually creates. A worn finish gives a piece more dimension and interest.

DECORATIVE FINISHES

FAUX FINISHING

color washing

Color washing is a sheer layer of color applied to raw wood or over a painted surface. If the surface has carvings or crevices, the color wash collects in those areas, adding to the dimensional look.

Color Washing Technique
If color washing on wood, sand with the grain until smooth and wipe away any dust. If color washing on a painted surface, base paint with 1-3 coats. Mix 1 to 2 parts Neutral Glaze with 1 part colored glaze or paint color. For a thinner, more transparent finish, add 1 teaspoon water to 4-6 oz. of glaze mix.

Using a Sponge
(Photo A)
Dampen a sponge and squeeze out the excess water. Dip the sponge into the glaze mixture. Pull and rub the sponge over the surface, smoothing the color as you go.

Using a Brush
(Photo B)
Brush technique: Dip the tips of the brush into the glaze mixture. Brush over the surface with long, smooth strokes. Use a damp cloth to periodically wipe excess glaze buildup from the bristles. The French Brush is ideal for applying color washes to crevices or carved areas.

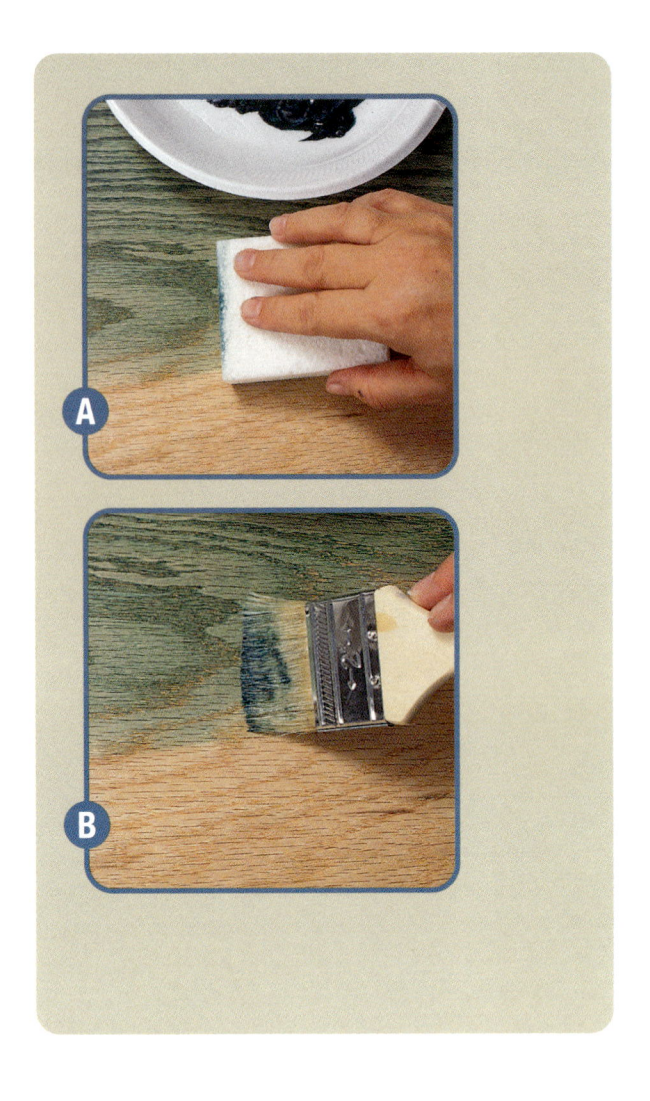

This dark gray wall has been color washed with gray and neutral glaze. The glaze was applied so that it settled more around the raised areas of the wood.

This wall is base coated with cobalt blue paint, then color washed with turquoise. The paint was allowed to settle in the crevices and brushed out over the smooth areas of the wood.

82 DECORATIVE FINISHES

FAUX FINISHING

color washing (continued)

The surface has been base coated with a medium purple paint. Color washing was achieved with a French Brush and dark purple glaze, using crosshatched brush strokes.

The background of this carved molding was painted cream; the raised areas were painted off-white. A darker glaze color was applied with the French Brush, allowing the glaze to settle into the carved areas. Glaze was then brushed diagonally over the lower portion of the wall to create texture.

DECORATIVE FINISHES | 83

FAUX FINISHING

crackling

What normally takes years of wind and weather can be created instantly with Crackle Medium. Crackle finishes can be achieved with one paint color or two, or Crackle Medium can be applied over raw wood so that the wood is exposed through the cracks.

Two-Color Technique
1. Using a foam brush, apply Crackle Medium over base painted surface and let dry. **(Photo A)** When the Crackle Medium is dry, there should be an overall sheen to the surface. If any areas appear dull, apply another coat.
2. Brush on an even, smooth coat of the topcoat paint color. **(Photo B)** Cracks will form. Do not over brush the area – over brushing will make the cracks disappear. Let dry.

One-Color Technique
(Photo C)
1. Follow instructions for steps 1 and 2 for Two-Color Crackle technique above, but use a water base varnish for the topcoat. Cracks will form. Do not over brush. Let dry completely.
2. To make the cracks more apparent, apply an antiquing mix of Neutral and colored Decorator Glaze to the surface, rubbing the glaze in with a damp sponge. Let dry.

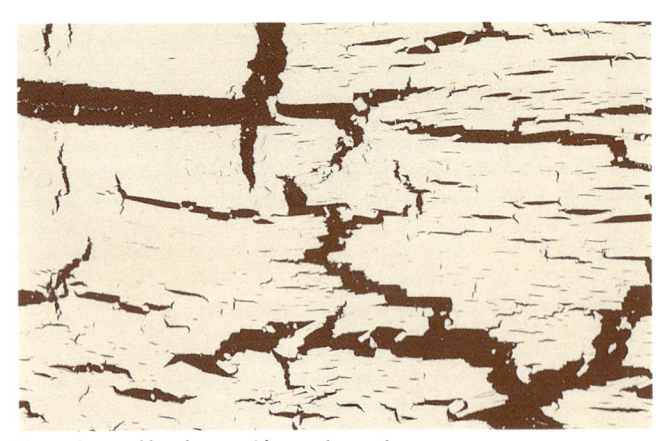

Two-color crackle—basecoat brown, top coat cream.

One-color crackle—basecoat Ivory and a dark brown antiquing finish.

DECORATIVE FINISHES

FAUX FINISHING

crackling (continued)

HELPFUL HINTS:

- Practice on smaller projects before tackling a larger project, such as a wall.

- When you begin to apply the topcoat, be sure everything is ready and use a container for the topcoat that is large enough to hold all the paint or varnish you'll need. (You won't have time to refill your container.)

- Use a lamp to illuminate the surface so it's easier to see where you've brushed.

- Apply enough of the topcoat—you can't go back and add more.

- Keep a wet edge when applying the topcoat so each stroke blends with the next.

- In general, a thicker topcoat creates bigger cracks; a thinner topcoat creates finer, smaller cracks.

- You can apply a thicker topcoat to horizontal surfaces; on a vertical surface, a thick topcoat can sag. When working on a piece of furniture, turn the piece and work one side at a time.

- If you like, you can use a painting pad to apply the topcoat to large areas, such as walls. Practice first on a piece of poster board.

- One-color crackle is an excellent technique for creating an aged look over surfaces that are stenciled, stamped, block printed, or painted with designs. Allow to dry, then apply Crackle Medium, then the Waterbase Varnish topcoat.

- Creating a Crusted Crackled Finish: A crusted crackle finish is a more primitive aged look. While the topcoat is still wet, use a bristle brush to lightly stroke random areas. This brushing will cause the surface to look rough and crusty.

Give a discarded table a new look with faux finishing. The original mahogony finish serves as the basecoat, stencil the design with crackle medium, let dry, and stencil the design again in the topcoat color. The legs and base feature the one-color technique.

DECORATIVE FINISHES 85

FAUX FINISHING

wood graining

Wood graining can make any paintable surface appear to be wood. This technique was widely used in 18th and 19th century homes to create the appearance of rare, costly woods on less expensive wood surfaces.

Wood Graining Technique

1. Apply base color. Apply a second base color over the first, randomly stroke the color on the surface with a French Brush or a sponge in the direction you're planning to create the wood grain. **(Photo A)** Let dry.
2. Mix equal amounts of colored glaze or paint and Neutral Glaze. Brush or roll the glaze mixture on the surface, working one area at a time. **(Photo B)**
3. While glaze is still wet, pull Wood Grainer through glaze. **(Photo C)** Rock the tool as you pull. Your grain will look better if you pull and rock the entire length of your area before lifting tool. If you stop, you'll create a line or mark. Do not roll it back and forth. Periodically wipe excess glaze from Wood Grainer with a damp cloth rag and a bristle brush. See package for additional instructions.
4. Again, while glaze is still wet, use the Flogging Brush to tap the surface and soften the lines and add fine detail lines that look like grain. **(Photo D)** Don't overwork the glaze.

Create the look of fine-grained wood with the Flogging Brush. Prepare glaze and apply to the basecoated surface with a foam brush or roller. While the glaze is still moist but not "wet," use the side of the Flogging Brush to "slap" the surface with the bristles.

86 | DECORATIVE FINISHES

FAUX FINISHING

wood graining (continued)

This faux-grained door was created with a light brown base coat and a dark brown glaze color. Achieve a more realistic-looking result by following the structure that a real wooden door would have.

DECORATIVE FINISHES

FAUX FINISHING

faux leather

The warm, natural look of leather is a wonderful addition to any room. Leather can be smooth, aged, wrinkled, burnished, or cracked – a faux leather finish can emulate each of these looks. Apply glaze using a positive or negative technique.

Positive Application Technique
1. Dampen Chamois Mitt. Remove excess water by blotting on rag or paper towel. Place some of your Decorator Glaze mixture in a disposable plate. Load Chamois Mitt by patting in the mixture that is in the disposable plate. **(Photo A)** To even out mixture on mitt, pat loaded mitt onto a second clean plate.
2. Pat mitt onto base painted project surface, varying your hand position. **(Photo B)**
3. Rub surface with Chamois Mitt to impart the look of age. This smooths the texture. The top right corner of closeup is patted. **(Photo C)** The left side shows the rubbing after patting. Allow glaze to slightly "set up" before rubbing.

Negative Application Technique
Working on one area at a time, apply glaze to the painted surface with a brush or roller. Moisten the Texturing Mitt and squeeze out excess water. Pat the glaze with the mitt to remove some of the glaze and create texture. Rinse the mitt periodically to prevent glaze buildup. For a worn look, use the mitt to pat and rub the glaze in random areas before it dries completely.

88   DECORATIVE FINISHES

FAUX FINISHING

faux leather (continued)

The comfortable look of faux leather can transform a room. To achieve this look, use the Texturing Mitt to apply a dark green glaze mixture over a blue-green basecoat.

DECORATIVE FINISHES | **89**

FAUX FINISHING

marbelizing

Faux marble can be realistic or freeform and fanciful. The marbleizing process can be layered and structured or simple and quick. The key to a beautiful faux marble finish is to remember to keep your work irregular, not patterned or uniform.

Marbelizing Technique

1. Base paint surface white, let dry. Mix off-white and Neutral Glaze. Pounce the mixture randomly over the wall with the Stippler Brush. **(Photo A)**
2. Pounce a darker glaze mixture randomly over the surface with the Stippler Brush. **(Photo B)**
3. Dilute white glaze with a small amount of water. Dip the edge of a feather in the glaze and drag it across the surface to create veins. **(Photo C)** Hold the feather over the surface to create veins. At times, wiggle the feather or shake your hand.
4. Dip feather and pull between the veins to create cracks. **(Photo D)**
5. Mist the surface lightly with water to soften the look and spatter lightly with the brown glaze mixture.

Practice on a piece of poster board before working on your project surface.

DECORATIVE FINISHES

FAUX FINISHING

marbelizing (continued)

HELPFUL HINTS:

- Allow some drifts and veins to fade out and disappear completely for a more authentic look.

- Most marble patterns have cracks created by shifts in the earth that bonded together again under pressure. Be sure your cracks are irregular, not shaped like Xs, Ys, or Zs.

- Some cracks should run the direction of the drifts and veins; make others perpendicular to them. When crossing a vein or drift, pick up the feather when you reach the vein or drift and reposition it on the other side, slightly shifting the crack up or down. Allow some cracks to be more vivid than others.

This lovely marbled foyer was created over a creamy yellow base coated wall. Darker yellow and white glaze mixtures were applied with the Stippler Brush. Veins and cracks were created with diluted dark yellow glaze.

DECORATIVE FINISHES

FAUX FINISHING

metal finishes

Faux metal looks are increasingly popular as the use of authentic metal in home décor increases. Almost any surface can be given a metal appearance.

Brushed Steel
To create the look of brushed steel, basecoat the surface with gray paint. Mix equal parts of silver metallic paint and Neutral glaze and equal parts of black paint and neutral glaze.

For a straight brush pattern, use the French Brush to apply long, smooth strokes of the silver metallic glaze mixture. Add a few strokes of black glaze mixture. Add a second application of silver metallic glaze, if desired.

For a swirled effect, apply silver metallic glaze to the surface in half-moon strokes with the French Brush (use 3/4" stencil brush for smaller swirls). For a deeper steel texture, do not mix Neutral glaze with the paint.

Aged Copper
To create the look of aged copper, paint the surface with bronze metallic paint, sanding between coats. Mix one part black, brown, and Neutral glaze and apply with the Stippler Brush. While the glaze is still wet, mist the surface with water until drips form. Tilt the surface in various directions so that the glaze runs and smears.

Brushed Copper
Base paint the surface with gold metallic paint. Let dry. Apply copper glaze with the Stippler Brush, laying the flat bristles on the surface and twisting your hand and wrist to create a swirl pattern. Let dry and repeat with gold glaze.

Oxidized Copper
Paint the surface with copper metallic paint, let dry. Mix equal parts of copper and neutral glaze and apply randomly to the surface with a damp sponge. Mix equal parts bright copper paint and neutral glaze and apply randomly with a damp sponge. Use a flat brush and blue paint to lightly stroke a patina around the edge of the surface as shown.

(From left to right) swirled black and silver metallic paint, swirled silver metallic paint, and brushed silver metallic paint.

Aged copper

Brushed copper

Oxidized copper

DECORATIVE FINISHES

FAUX FINISHING

metal finishes (continued)

This brushed steel chair was created with the French Brush and a 3/4" stencil brush and a silver metallic glaze mixture.

DECORATIVE FINISHES

FAUX FINISHING

stone and brick effects

The look of brick and natural stone are beautiful textures for walls and other surfaces. Brick walls and floors are easily created with grout tape and sponging. Travertine stone uses stippling, flogging and spattering to create an authentic-looking faux surface. Granite, a stone finish with a uniform texture, can be created with sponging and spattering.

Brick Technique

1. Base paint surface. Let dry completely. Mark a grid for placing the bricks on the surface, making bricks 2¼" x 7¾". Use a plumb line and a level to be sure lines are level and straight. On a floor, use a chalk line to mark straight lines. Tape off mortar lines with Grout Tape. **(Photo A)**
2. Load Stippler Brush or French Brush with one of the stippling colors. Pounce bristles to distribute paint. Stipple surface. **(Photo B)**
3. Stipple next color or colors, placing colors randomly for a natural look. **(Photo C)** Wipe the brush bristles on a damp cloth when changing colors to avoid mixing the paints and getting a muddy look.
4. Remove the grout tape and let the surface dry completely.

Options

For a weathered look, lightly mist the surface with water. Moisten a sponge and dip lightly in mortar color. Pounce sponge to distribute color, then pounce color sparingly on surface.

For a mossy look, use the "weathered look" technique with a green paint color. Sponge bricks before or after Grout Tape is removed.

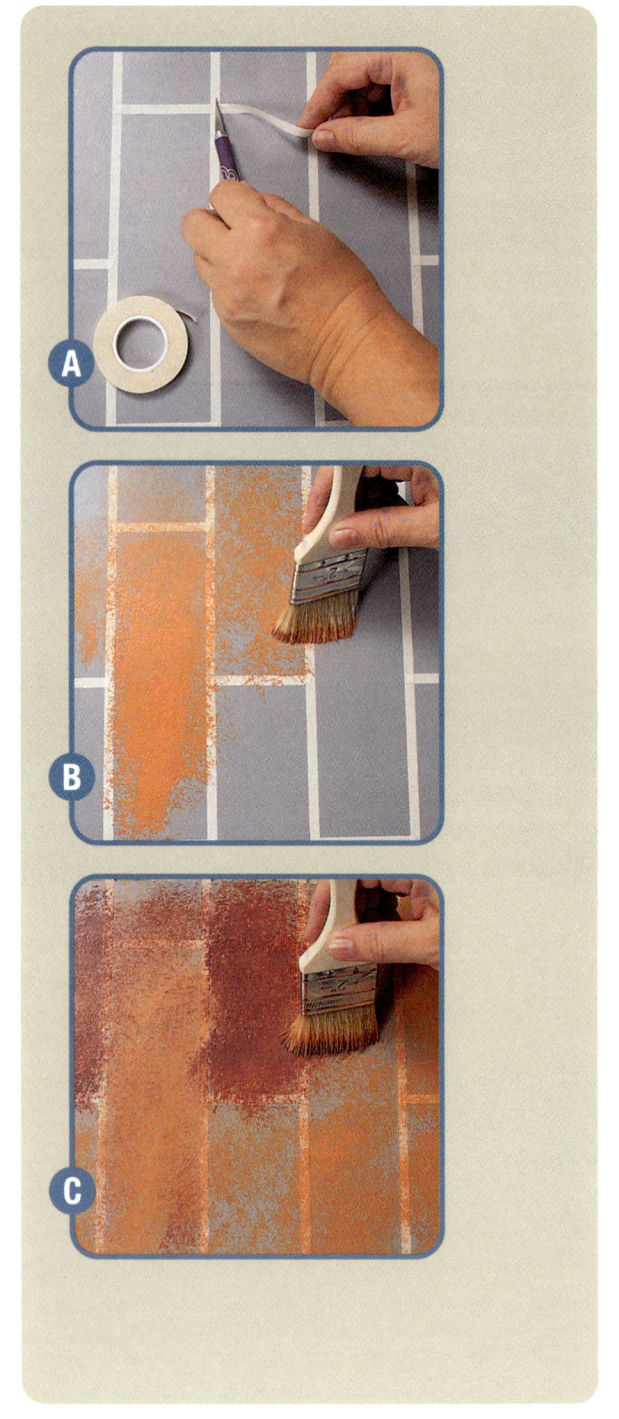

94 DECORATIVE FINISHES

FAUX FINISHING

stone and brick effects (continued)

HELPFUL HINTS:

- Start marking and measuring on the most noticeable wall and work around from both sides to the least noticeable area of the room. If you start in the center, then the blocks will end up in the same position at the left and right corners.

- If the tape is not secure, especially at corners, glaze can bleed under the tape. (On large projects, this is bound to happen occasionally.) If this happens, use a wet cotton swab to rub away the excess glaze or use a small artist's brush with the wall paint color to paint over the glaze bleed.

- Remove the tape slowly. Do not pull at it from a distance—stay close and remove the tape carefully. This will help prevent damage to the wall or the glaze.

- Separate brushes can be used for each glaze color. This will keep you from having to wipe the brush constantly when changing colors and will make the job go more quickly.

DECORATIVE FINISHES

FAUX FINISHING

stone and brick effects (continued)

Blue Granite
To create the look of Blue Bahia granite, basecoat the wall in dark blue. Sponge the basecoated wall with a mix of equal parts black and neutral glaze, allowing some of the background color to show through. Let dry. Lightly sponge the wall with a mix of equal parts sky blue and neutral wall glaze, let dry. Spatter the wall with diluted glaze mixes.

Travertine Roman Stone
Travertine Roman stone is created over a limestone-colored basecoat. Use the tips of the French Brush to apply mushroom glaze, stroking and brushing over the surface. While the glaze is still wet, pounce and stroke the surface with camel and dark brown glazes. Maintaining a linear pattern, pounce the wet glaze with the side of the Flogging Brush bristles to mellow the colors. Mist with water from time to time to keep the surface moist. Spatter the surface with diluted brown glaze mixture; diffuse the spatters with the Flogging Brush.

Create dark, elongated patterns on the surface by dipping the handle of the French Brush in dark brown glaze and touching it to the surface, sliding slightly. Pounce the marks with the French Brush to soften.

Blue granite.

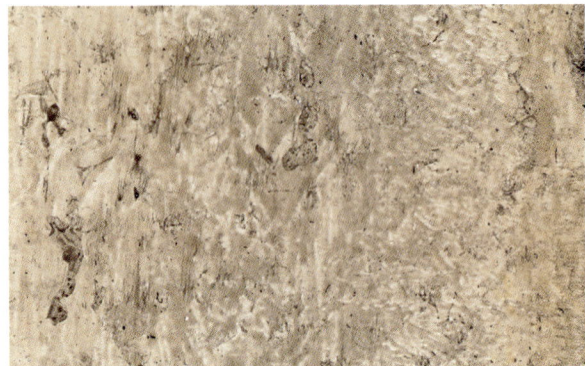

Travertine roman stone.

FAUX FINISHING

stone and brick effects (continued)

Grout tape is used with stippling to give these walls the old world look of cut stone blocks. The wall is painted with the color intended as the mortar color; two glaze colors give dimension to the blocks. Variations in color and texture are achieved by varying the stippling technique, color mix, and amount of glaze used.

FAUX FINISHING

colorways

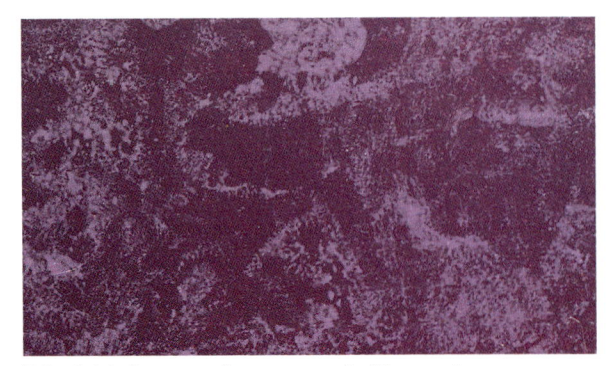

Pale violet glaze ragged over an eggplant basecoat.

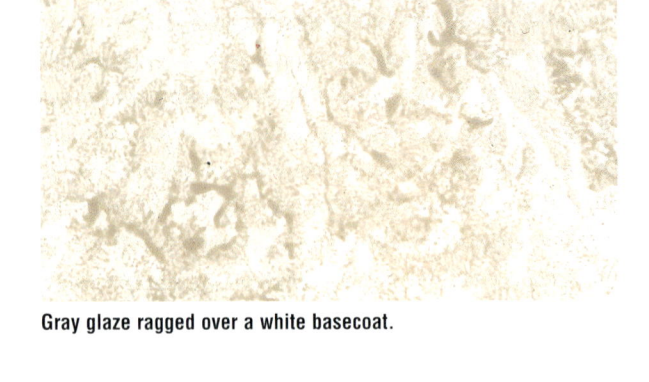

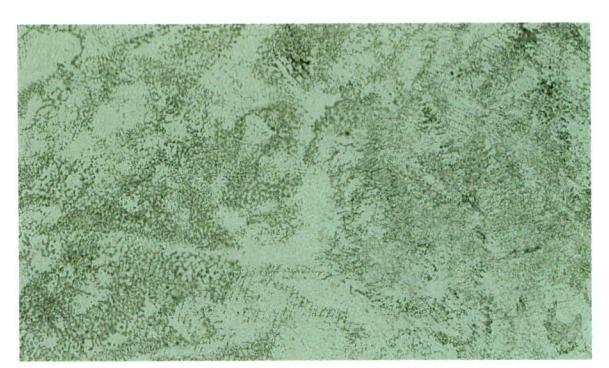

Gray glaze ragged over a white basecoat.

Light green basecoat ragged with deep green glaze.

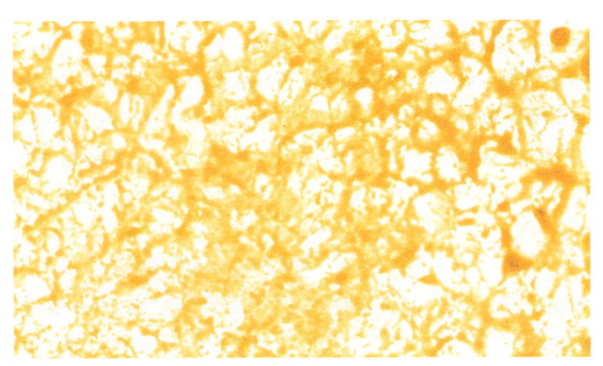

Yellow glaze sponged over a white basecoat.

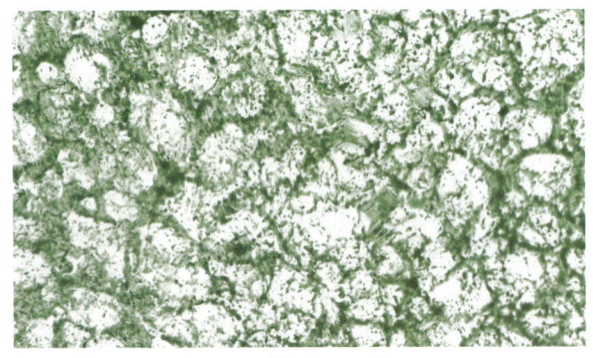

Green glaze sponged over a white basecoat.

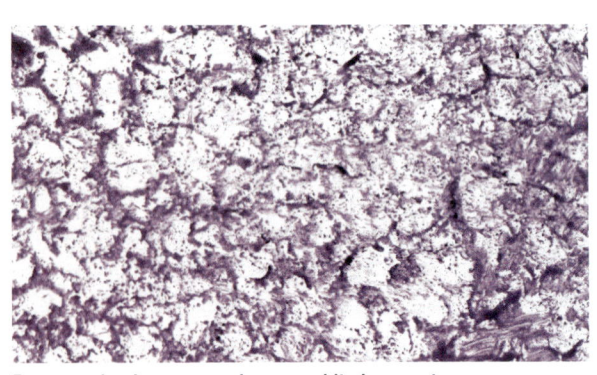

Deep purple glaze sponged over a white basecoat.

Red-orange glaze mopped over an apricot basecoat.

Burgundy glaze mopped over a wine-colored basecoat.

FAUX FINISHING

colorways (continued)

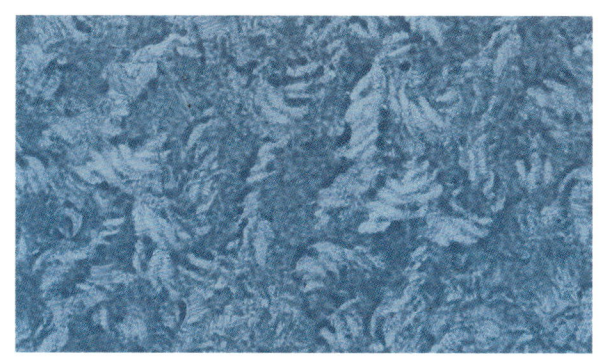

Damask blue basecoat mopped with medium blue glaze.

White basecoat brushed with pale blue glaze in a spiral motion.

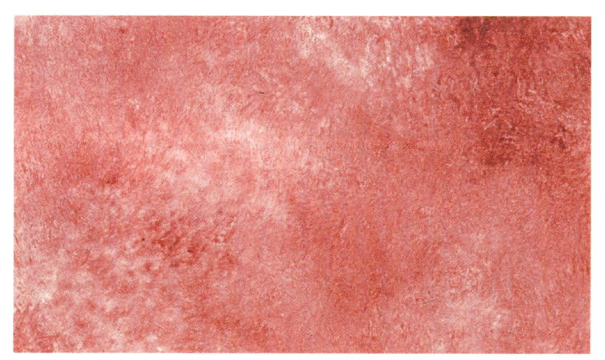

White basecoat stippled with red glaze.

Rust basecoat stippled with sunflower glaze.

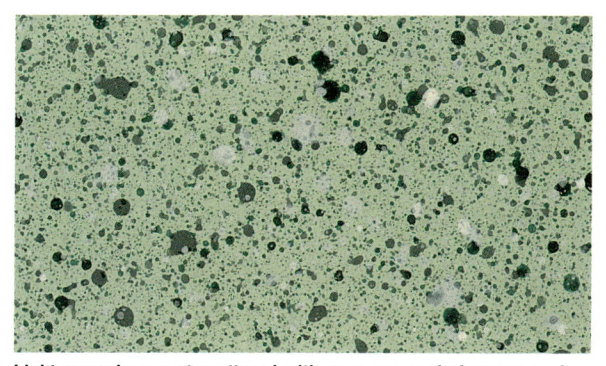

Light green basecoat spattered with sage green, dark green, and white glazes.

White basecoat spattered with sunflower glaze.

Off-white glaze brushed over a royal blue basecoat.

Medium brown basecoat combed with dark brown glaze and pounced with the flogging brush.

DECORATIVE FINISHES

FAUX FINISHING

colorways (continued)

Tan basecoat with camel inset, combed with dark gray glaze. Ferns stenciled with olive glaze.

Damask blue basecoat combed with navy glaze.

Green glaze applied over a raw wood surface.

Tan glaze applied over a sable brown basecoat.

Spring green glaze washed over a raw wood surface.

Pearl white glaze applied over an aqua basecoat.

Crackle Medium over a green and tan basecoat; topcoated wtih matte varnish and rubbed with brown glaze.

Crackle Medium applied over a dark blue basecoat; topcoated with light blue and rubbed with brown glaze.

FAUX FINISHING

colorways (continued)

Dark brown glaze applied with the chamois mitt over a light brown basecoat.

White glaze applied with the french brush, sponge, and feather over a black basecoat.

Rust, dark brown and white glazes applied with a stippler brush, sponge, and feather.

Rusted iron effect created with red, yellow, and brown glazes sponged and stippled over a red-orange basecoat.

Steel effect created with silver, light blue, red and brown glazes sponged and stippled over a gray basecoat.

Stone tiles created with medium brown and light gold glazes sponged over a cream basecoat.

DECORATIVE FINISHES

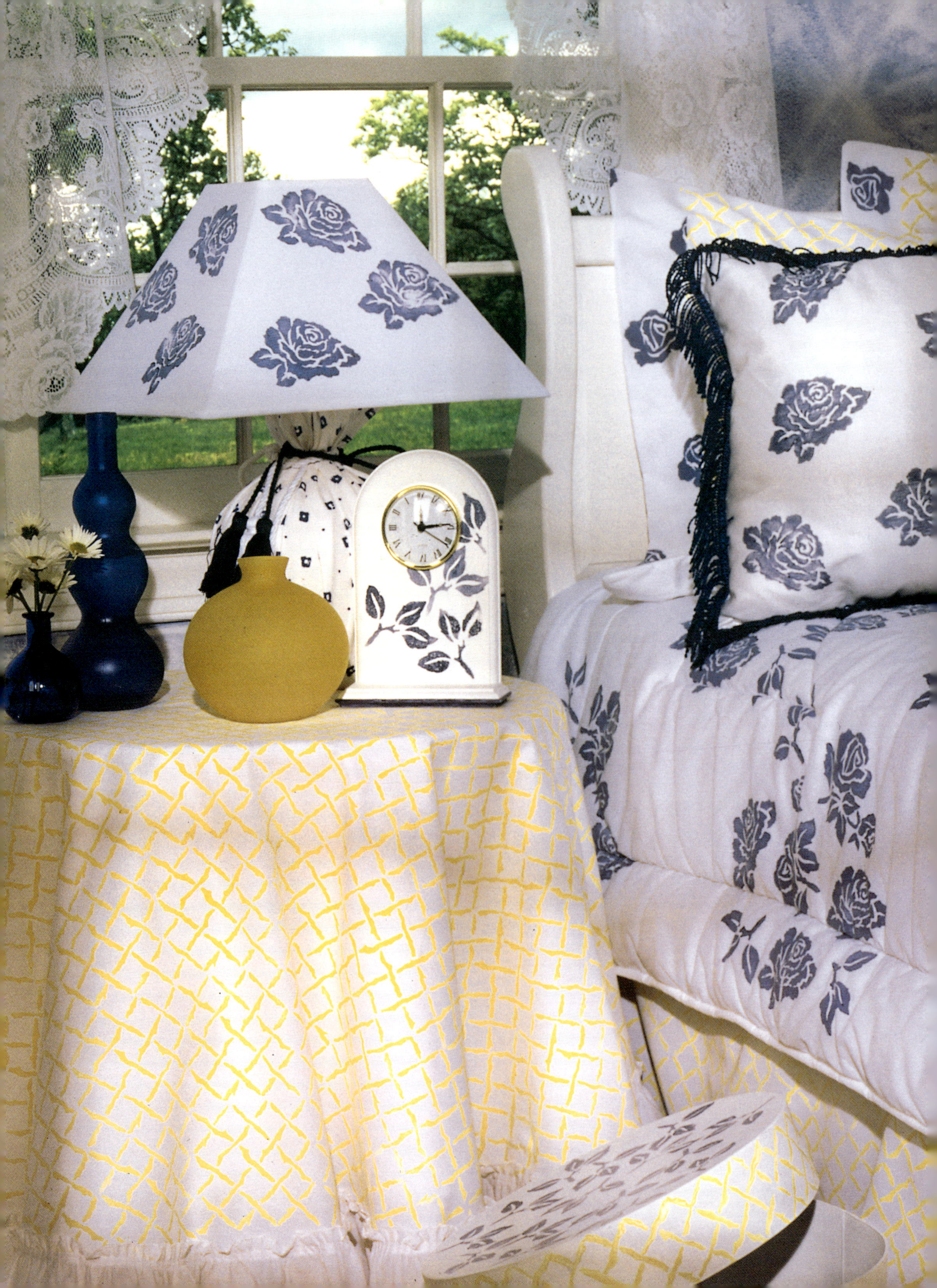

STAMPING

Stamping is a time-honored method of applying form and color to surfaces. In this technique, paint or glaze is applied to a pre-cut foam or rubber stamp; the stamp is then pressed onto the surface to create an image. Throughout history, examples of stamped designs have been found on walls, textiles, books, games and furniture. Today, it's simple to create beautiful stamped designs on a variety of surfaces with a few simple tools.

Stamping is an especially easy way to add interest to walls, furnishings, and home accessories. Your finished design can be as simple or intricate as you desire – stamping looks great on its own, or it can be combined with faux finishing or other backgrounds for spectacular effects. Reverse, tone-on-tone, and shadow stamping techniques offer even more ways to be creative. In this section, you'll find ideas and instructions for a variety of stamping techniques. Have fun experimenting with them and add your own personal touch for a unique result!

DECORATIVE FINISHES

STAMPING

tools and materials

Stamps
Stamps are available in a wide range of sizes and design themes. Smaller stamps can be used to create accents of repeated patterns, while larger stamps can transform an entire room. Look for stamps that complement stenciled or faux finished surfaces —several Stamp Decor™ designs from Plaid feature coordinating stencil designs.

Paint
Select a paint that matches your stamp design and the surface you are working with. Virtually any type of paint can be used for stamping, so let permanency, transparency and sheen be your guide to the best paint for the project. (See page 14 for details on paints.)

Brushes and Applicators
There are several tools that may be used to load paint onto the stamp surface. Foam rollers offer quick and easy application. Flat paintbrushes offer more precise loading and can be used to load multiple colors. A cosmetic or cellulose sponge works well, and stamps can also be loaded directly from a paint palette or foam plate.

Additional Tools and Materials
Paper or foam plates for a disposable and readily accessible palette
Paper towels for cleanup
Chalk pencil for marking fabrics and walls
Yardstick, measuring tape, bubble (carpenter's) level and plumb line.
Ladder

104 DECORATIVE FINISHES

STAMPING

single-color loading

There are several ways to load stamps with Decorator Glaze. Before stamping, always make a test print on a surface similar to that of your project.

Palette
(Photo A)
Squeeze out a small amount of glaze or paint on to a large foam plate and spread it evenly over the plate with a craft stick or putty knife. Place the stamp in the glaze and press lightly. Lift the stamp off of the plate.

Foam Roller
(Photo B)
Moisten the roller; towel dry. Squeeze glaze or paint onto a palette or disposable plate. Move the roller back and forth in the glaze to disperse it evenly through the roller. Holding the stamp in the palm of your hand, gently roll glaze from edge to edge of the stamp. Avoid pressing too firmly – this will force glaze into the crevices of the stamp, resulting in a poor print.

DECORATIVE FINISHES | 105

STAMPING

multi-color loading

There are several ways to load stamps with Decorator Glaze. Before stamping, always make a test print on a surface similar to that of your project.

Foam Roller
(Photos A and B)

Use two rollers to load separate colors onto the stamp, or squeeze small amounts of glaze next to each other on a plate and roll one roller through both colors. Be careful not to over-blend the colors on the roller. Load the stamp.

Brush
(Photo C)

Load the first glaze color onto the stamp. Using a clean brush, add a second glaze color.

DECORATIVE FINISHES

how to stamp

Stamping Technique

Once you've loaded glaze or paint onto the stamp, you're ready to apply it to your project surface.

1. Hold the loaded stamp by its handle and position on the surface. Press. **(Photo A)**
2. Release the handle and press on the back of the stamp, from the center outward. Use your fingers, not the heel of your hand, for consistent pressure over the stamp. **(Photo B)**
3. Lift the stamp off the surface, using the handle. Be careful to lift the stamp straight up to prevent smearing the stamped image. **(Photo C)**

Clean stamps before glaze or paint dries to prevent damage to the stamp. To clean, moisten the stamp with water and brush with a soft-bristle toothbrush dipped in mild soap. Rinse clean and allow the stamp to dry thoroughly, cut side up. Store stamps loosely in a plastic bag. Do not soak stamps in water.

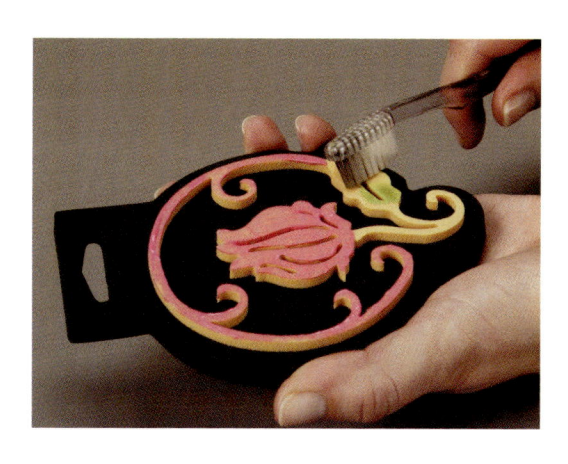

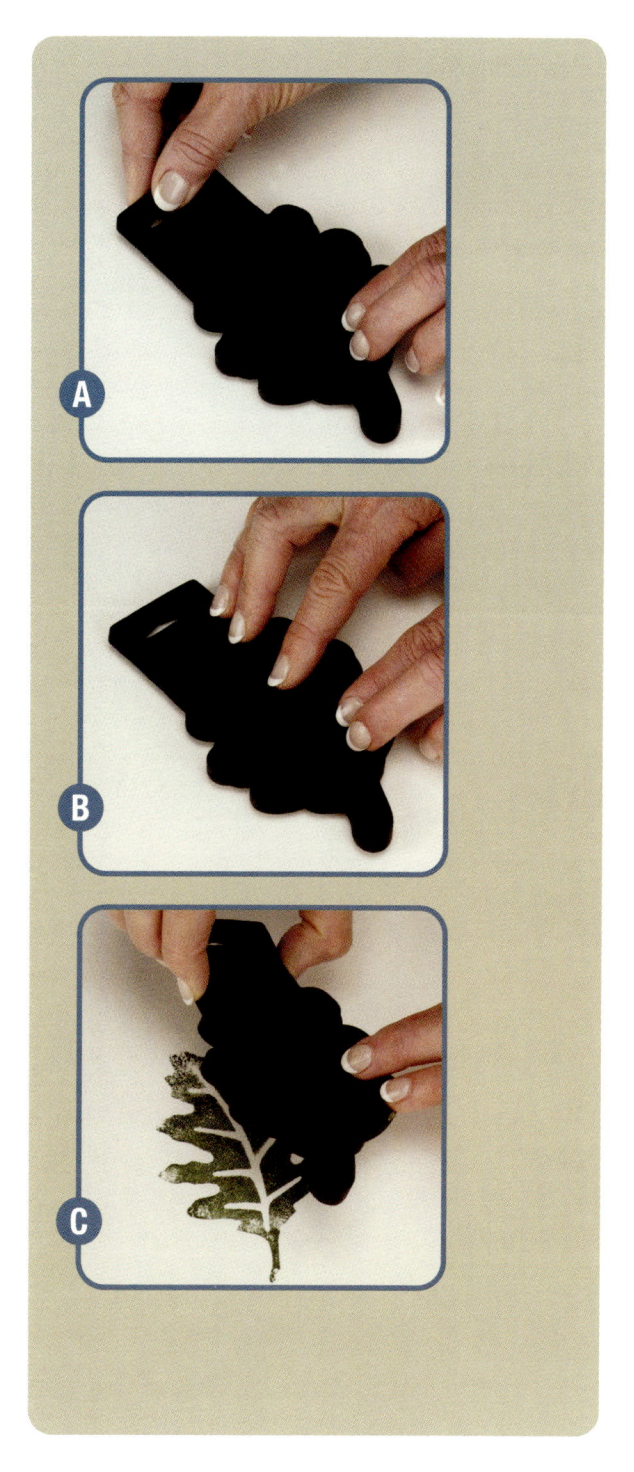

STAMPING

DECORATIVE FINISHES 107

STAMPING

easy projects

Fern chests: show a combination of stamping and spattering. Stamp image first then spatter over entire surface. Edges of chest are done by watering down paint and wiping onto surface to create a worn look.

STAMPING

easy projects (continued)

Time-worn rose: rose stamp design shows how-to crackle using a stamped impression. Edges of wood bench were highlighted using a paste gold leaf paint to give that worn look to the painted finish.

DECORATIVE FINISHES

STAMPING

creative stamping

Although the basic technique is quick and easy, your stamped results can be as simple or sophisticated as you wish! Following are a few ideas for creating special effects with stamps.

Basic Stamping
(Photo A)
Roll or brush color onto the stamp and apply to the surface. Remember that each successive application will be lighter.

Multi-Color Stamping
(Photo B)
Brush two or more colors onto the stamp, or roll a stencil roller though two colors on the palette, then apply to the stamp for a variegated or shadowed effect.

A

B

Basic stamping.

Multi-color stamping.

DECORATIVE FINISHES

STAMPING

creative stamping (continued)

Aged Effect
(Photo A)

Apply paint to stamp and make the first impression on a piece of scrap paper before stamping on the project surface.

Visual Texture
(Photo B)

Load the stamp, then press it onto a textured surface such as a paper towel or woven cloth. Press the stamp onto the project surface to create a textured effect.

Aged effect.

Visual texture.

DECORATIVE FINISHES | 111

STAMPING

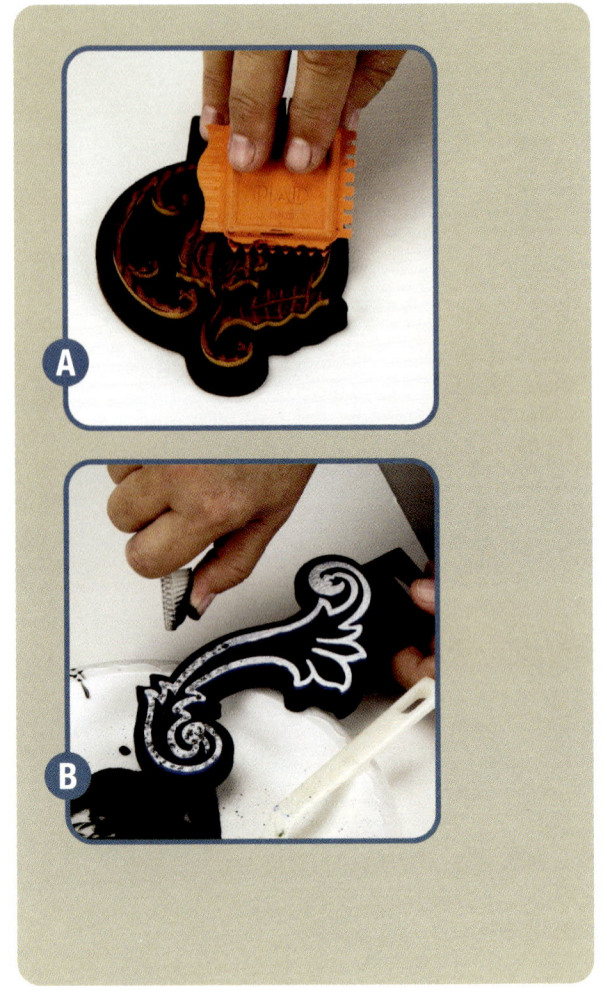

creative stamping (continued)

Streak Effect
(Photo A)
Load the stamp and lightly swipe a French Brush or combing tool across the surface, leaving a series of parallel lines in the paint. Stamp onto the project surface for a streaked look.

Variegated Effect
(Photo B)
Load the stamp, and while it is still wet, spatter a contrasting or coordinating color over the stamp's surface. Press it onto the project surface for a faux effect.

Streak effect.

Variegated effect.

112 | DECORATIVE FINISHES

STAMPING

creative stamping (continued)

Fossil Effect
(Photo A)

This technique is applied to a wet glazed surface. Use a stencil roller to apply a thin layer of water or rubbing alcohol to the stamp. Press the stamp into the wet surface and lift up, creating a faded negative image.

Vintage Effect
(Photo B)

For a vintage look, load the stamp with a mixture of equal parts paint and neutral glaze. Press the stamp to the project surface several times before reloading for a natural look.

Fossil effect.

Vintage effect.

DECORATIVE FINISHES | 113

STAMPING

stamping borders

Aligning a Border

Using a spacer card between design repeats is an easy way to stamp rows of prints horizontally or vertically. Cut the spacer from stiff cardstock or a file folder.

1. Use a level and pencil to mark a horizontal line for the border. **(Photo A)** Use paper proofs to determine the distance between each design repeat. Cut the spacer to this width.
2. Stamp the first image. Using the card as a measurement tool, mark the placement for the second image. **(Photo B)**
3. Stamp the second image. Mark and stamp the consecutive images. **(Photo C)**
4. Erase the pencil marks. **(Photo D)**

Continuous Border

To make a continuous border, mark the center of the stamp horizontally and vertically with a permanent marker. Decide where you want the center of the stamped design to fall on the wall; mark this line on the wall using a level and chalk pencil. Load the stamp and press it onto the wall, aligning the center mark on back of the stamp with the line on wall.

DECORATIVE FINISHES

STAMPING

stamping on borders (continued)

DECORATIVE FINISHES | 115

STAMPING

stamping on walls

Full Wall Measurement

Achieving a symmetrical design on a wall or other large surface is easy when you create a simple measurement tool. A template will allow precise horizontal and vertical placement of each image.

To make a template card, cut a 12" square from heavy cardstock or a file folder. (Standard spacing for full wall diagonal placement is generally 10"–12" between vertical rows.) Draw intersecting lines from corner to corner on the template.

1. Beginning 6" from the corner, mark a vertical line on the wall from floor to ceiling with a level and pencil. **(Photo A)**
2. Align the template over the marked line, dropping the card down from the ceiling line about half the height of the design motif (this will allow room for the first motif to start about 1" from the ceiling). Mark the wall at each corner of the card. **(Photo B)** Drop the template down along the marked line, matching the bottom marking to the top of the template and marking the wall until the placement for the lowest design is marked. Move the card horizontally and vertically, aligning the template with previous marks.
3. Stamp the design, centering the motif over each mark. **(Photo C)**

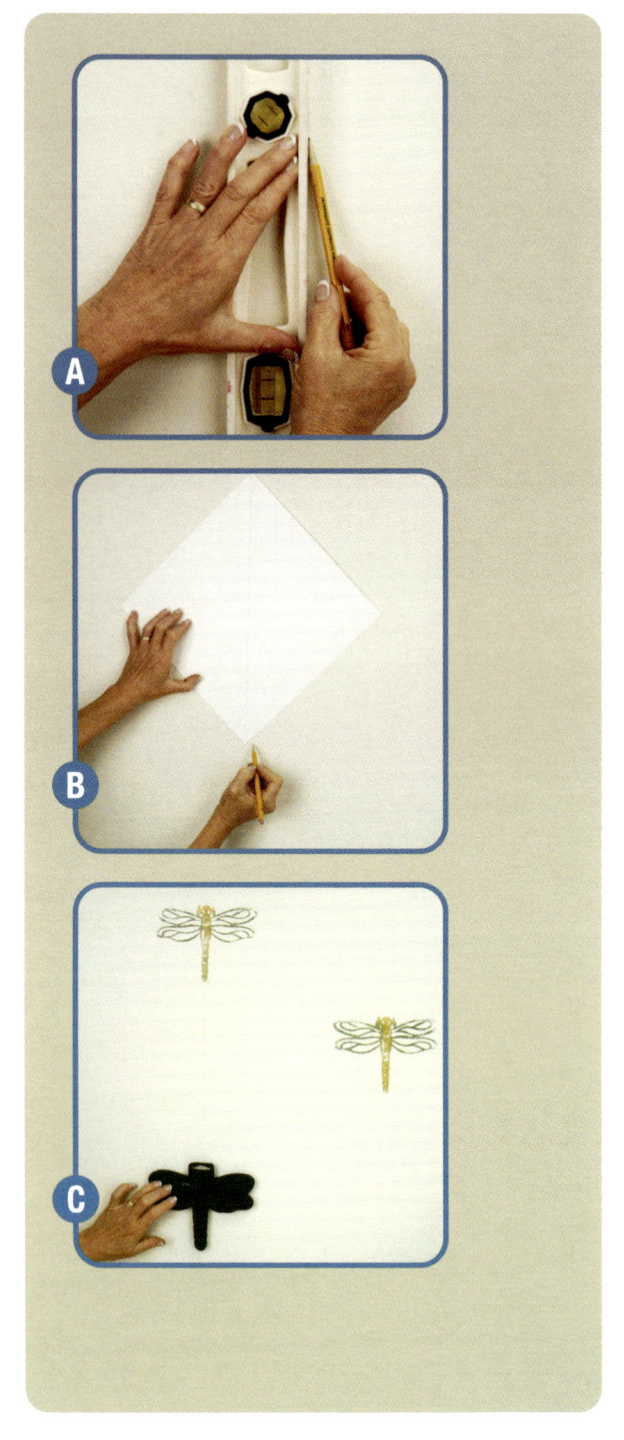

> For a random design, use adhesive notes on the wall for stamp placement, adjust to your liking. Remove paper and stamp design one at a time until project is complete.

A

B

C

116 DECORATIVE FINISHES

STAMPING

stamping on walls (continued)

Stamping on Dark Surfaces
Dark surfaces can offer a dramatic background for a stamped image. Follow these easy steps for a clear, vivid impression.
1. Prepare the surface and paint the basecoat color; let dry.
2. Load the stamp with a white or off-white acrylic paint. Stamp on the surface and let dry.
3. Make a paper proof of the design and tape it to the back of the stamp. Load the stamp with glaze or paint and stamp over the first image, using the proof as a placement guide. If desired, slightly offset the stamped image for a drop shadow effect.

DECORATIVE FINISHES 117

STAMPING

fabric surfaces

It's easy to create custom fabrics and coordinated accessories with stamps. A few basic guidelines will ensure a crisp, lasting result.

Stamping on Fabric

1. Wash and dry fabric before stamping. Do not use fabric softener. Press out any wrinkles and place blank newsprint or paper underneath to serve as a blotter.
2. Load the stamp, taking care not to apply too much glaze. Test the print by stamping on a hidden area of the fabric, or on a scrap fabric of similar material. If the imprint is too heavy, first stamp on a piece of scrap paper to offload excess paint.
3. Allow your stamped project to air dry for 24 hours. Do not fold or stack fabric pieces.
4. If you make a mistake, do not attempt to wash it out. Stamp again over the mistake to camouflage it. Slight smudges may be removable with an artists' eraser before the piece is heat set.
5. Heat set the design with an iron set on wool. Do not use steam. Cover the stamped print with a pressing cloth, place the iron on the cloth, and hold it over the stamped design for 30 seconds. For larger pieces, tumble in a hot drier for 30 minutes before heat setting with the iron.
6. Launder or dry clean stamped fabrics according to the manufacturer's instructions.

DECORATIVE FINISHES

STAMPING

fabric surfaces (continued)

DECORATIVE FINISHES | 119

STAMPING

floors

A stamped design adds a unique, personal touch to a porch, patio, or bedroom. Planning and preparation are important keys to success.

Surface Preparation
Be sure the floor is smooth and free of dust and dirt. Stain or paint the floor, allowing the finish to dry between coats. Let dry. Before stamping, seal the floor with a clear acrylic sealer – this will allow you to remove smudges or mistakes without staining the base color.

Planning Design
For a random stamped design, stamp paper proofs and arrange them on the floor in the desired position. For a symmetrical or striped design, find the center of the floor by measuring diagonally from the corners. Measure and mark the pattern from the center of the floor to the edges to ensure a balanced look.

Stamping the Design
Use paper proofs to help you visualize spacing and lightly mark the floor with a chalk pencil to plan the layout.

To achieve a natural, freeform look, less is often better. You can always go back and add an element here or there to fill in a spot that looks empty.

Periodically stand back and look at the area to gauge the overall effect.

When working with several stamps at one time, place them face down on a damp towel to keep them from drying out.

Wear knee pads when working.

Let your stamped design dry for 24-36 hours.

Finishing
Wipe the floor to remove dust and dirt. Erase any markings with an artists' eraser.

Roll or brush on a thin coat of waterbase urethane sealer, using caution not to overwork the sealer, which could cause the glaze to bleed. Let dry.

Apply a second, heavier coat of sealer and let dry. Lightly sand the surface with a crumpled paper bag or #000 steel wool. Wipe the surface clean.

Apply third and fourth coats of sealer.

Don't want to paint directly on your floor? Look for solid color rugs, and inexpensive vinyl flooring scraps. Paint on the back side of linoleum, it's a great surface just basecoat with a primer first.

DECORATIVE FINISHES

STAMPING

furniture and other surfaces

STAMPING

furniture and other surfaces (continued)

This simple yet elegant chest of drawers features a whitewashed basecoat and a checkerboard stencil pattern that offsets the leaf design. Be sure to sand and seal wood surfaces before stamping.

122 DECORATIVE FINISHES

STAMPING

furniture and other surfaces (continued)

A single stamp motif can be used on several pieces to create a themed room setting. Mix and match surfaces, backgrounds and colors for visual appeal.

DECORATIVE FINISHES | 123

PHOTO GALLERY

124 DECORATIVE FINISHES

PHOTO GALLERY

DECORATIVE FINISHES 125

PHOTO GALLERY

126 DECORATIVE FINISHES

PHOTO GALLERY

DECORATIVE FINISHES 127

GLOSSARY

ACRYLIC
A water-based plastic polymer that acts as the binder in acrylic paints.

ANTIQUING
Any technique used to make a painted surface look old, usually refers to a thin glaze that is applied to a surface, allowing the undercoat to show through.

BLEEDING
Paint that seeps under the edge of a stencil.

BORDER
A repeating band of stencils that can be positioned at any height and on almost any surface.

BRIDGES
Narrow strips between open areas of a stencil that hold it together.

COLOR WASHING
Random layers of thin glaze that are blended to produce a faded, uneven look similar to that of whitewash or distemper.

COMBING
Any paint technique that involves marking narrow lines of color on a surface. Also called strié or dragging. Combing techniques that specifically intend to imitate wood are called wood graining techniques.

CRACKLE FINISH
A finish that cracks as it dries and gives an aged appearance.

DISTRESSED TECHNIQUE
Makes a surface appear to be older than it is.

FAUX
French for "false"—used to describe any technique in which paint imitates another substance, such as wood or stone.

GLAZE
A paint or colorant mixed with a transparent medium and diluted with a thinner compatible with the medium.

MASK
To apply protection around a stencil to prevent overspray.

MULTIPLE-LAYER STENCIL
A stenciled design that uses more than one stencil.

NEGATIVE TECHNIQUE
Any decorative painting technique that involves removing paint from a surface while it is still wet. *See also Positive technique.*

POSITIVE TECHNIQUE
Any painting technique that involves adding paint to a surface. *See also Negative technique.*

RAGGING
Using rags to create various decorative paint finishes in either a positive or negative application.

SEA SPONGE
The fibrous connective structure of a sea creature, used to apply and remove paint. Not to be confused with the cellulose variety used in household chores.

SINGLE-LAYER STENCIL
A stencil design that uses only one stencil.

SPATTERING
The technique of applying random dots of paint over a surface by striking a saturated brush or rubbing paint through a screen.

SPONGING
A paint technique that uses a natural sea sponge to put paint on or take paint off a surface.

STENCIL
A cut-out pattern that allows you to paint the same motif over and over. Complex stencils will have several overlapping patterns, and different colors are applied in layers after the previous coat dries.

STIPPLING
A stenciling method in which paint is applied in an up-and-down pouncing motion to produce textured results.

TROMPE L'OEIL
Literally, something that fools the eye. A painted scene or effect that simulates real life.

WASH
A thinned-out latex or acrylic paint.

WOOD GRAINING
A painting technique that seeks to resemble wood by imitating the lines found in cut lumber (which are the tree's growth rings).